WALKING THE LANES WITH LIZ

The Diaries of a Youthful Artist

by

JOHN TAYLOR
1875 - 1940

Edited by his Granddaughter

ANNE T. TAYLOR

FOR GEORGE -
from anne T &m
NEG TAYLOR.

Published by Theresa Michael
6 Marlborough Road
Bedford
MK40 4LG

All illustrations by John Taylor

Produced and printed by members of
THE GUILD OF MASTER CRAFTSMEN

Book Design and Typesetting by Cecil Smith

To order further copies of this book contact publisher

Printed and bound in Great Britain by
RPM PRINT & DESIGN
2-3 Spur Road, Quarry Lane, Chichester, West Sussex PO19 8PR

Contents

Self portrait by John Taylor 1897

Introduction.

At Christmas of 1986 my daughter gave my Aunt Marian a crib set, and after the feast was over my aunt turned out to top of her cupboard to make room for the crib figures and Stable. I came to lunch one Tuesday and she said "You might like to have those, I'd forgotten I had them." Inside the packet were five small notebooks and two sketchbooks that had been used by my grandfather John Taylor. The four main books are diaries, starting in May 1892, and petering out at the turn of the 1900's.

The fifth little notebook is a sort of story summary of the courtship between John and his future wife. The Sketch books have many drawings, some of friends, some landscapes and some drawings of hand or legs in various poses. There are also lots of tiny drawings in amongst the text of the diaries.

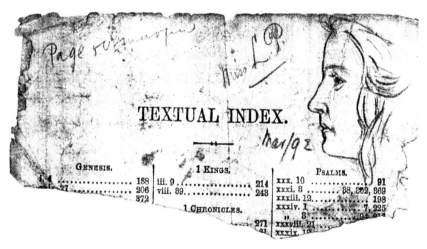

Among them is this tiny sketch on the flyleaf of a bible, just a tiny slip of paper that sums up John's loves, Art, Christ, and Lizzie Pugmire. John Taylor was born in November 1875, the youngest son, and second youngest child of the eleven children, born to Thomas Taylor, a blacksmith, and writer, and his wife Isabella nee Leathard. Thomas wrote several columns in the Newcastle Chronicle for over forty years. Isabella was known in the village as the person to call in any emergency, she was a good nurse, and could always cope calmly, she made her own ointments etc. The family lived in Dunston, a village which has now become part of Gateshead, although in the parish of Whickham in County Durham.

By the time John began writing, he was 16, and two of his brothers Tom and Bob) and one sister (Kate) were already married and living nearby, and one brother had died in infancy so the family at home was mainly sisters, Bella, Maggie, Minnie, Edward, & Ada, all older then John, and Lily the youngest of all.

At this time John was working as a clerk in the Dunston Engine Works or "Archer's", which was on the edge of the Tyne looking across towards the shipbuilding works of Armstrongs, over the river in Elswick, to the west of Newcastle upon Tyne. He was also attending the Gateshead School of Art and was very artistic, always painting and never with out a pencil and sketchbook in his pocket. The family attended the Ravensworth Road, Methodist New Connexion Chapel. Several of John's sisters were teachers at the local Board Schools, and his future wife was there also as a pupil teacher.

I have placed the notebook, first in this book because John gives a very full introduction to himself and the other people who appear in the diaries most frequently. I have cut quite a lot of the notebook because it is all covered at the dates it actually happened when John quotes from the note book. The spelling and punctuation are John's own including the underlining. I have broken up some of the entries into paragraphs, where John just wrote page after page. After the notebook, the first diary starts in May 1892. I have added some of the drawings from the sketch books, where they seem to fit in and illustrate the text, but most of the sketches are from the diaries.

The Diaries fizzle out at the turn of the century, after 1900 there are only major family events, lists of pictures etc. that brought in cash and lists of his salary increases over the years.

Anne T. Taylor (John's eldest grandchild..)

The Notebook

I Know a Maid
(Written specially, and dedicated, without her permission, to the
girl who outside our own family circle is dearest to my heart.)

I know a maid, a maid so fair–
With laughing eyes of colour rare
That sparkle bright, in liquid blue,
And ever dance with mischief new;
No matter when or where the place,
'Tis scarcely absent from her face.
She seems at all times blithe and free,
And always brimful filled with glee.
Yet from those orbs so sweet & clear
I've seen the mirth die out, A teardrop
Take its place.
Anon they dreamy gaze in space
Which tends to beautify her face–
A face that's pure, serene and sweet,
And one with which we rarely meet;
No classic line makes cold her feature;
Her face declares a loving nature.
A wealth of silken light brown hair,
Crowns high her shapely forehead fair,
And falls, unchecked, with simple taste,
Down to her slim and slender waist,
Shimmering with sheen like burnished gold;
So rich– so pleasing to behold!
In face– in every feature sweet,
In figure, grace itself Complete.
Her dress artistic taste displays,
Her very walk is full of grace.

She has a tongue, and O! how pert,
And quick in giving sharp retort!
In comprehension quick and clear;
Nothing address'd her,'scapes her ear;
And as for brilliant Conversation,
No girl can beat her in the nation;
Once start a subject that you've read,
And she will follow up the thread.
She's fond of walking , too, I know,
For lanes she roves in sleet or snow,
In March's wind or April showers,
This maid is found in evening's hours
Vacations are spent "up the lane",
Nor does she rove and roam in vain;
For there she must attraction find,
Attraction of another kind.
I've said enough, so now I'll end,
But first I fain would here append;
She's like an angel from above,
And this is she- The girl I love!

People say that I am mad, that I am a fool, that I am demented, soft, daft and all manner of evil is railed against me – and Why? Because I choose to associate with a good little girl of my acquaintance.

Before I go further, let me state my case briefly. Yet even before this, I will attempt to describe myself – to picture to whatever stranger having the nerve to read this (with my permission) what sort of a creature, what kind of a being am I, John Taylor age (August 1893) 17 2 /3 years.

Face rather oval, but inclined to be square, dark brown straight hair, eye-brows, & brown (dark) eyes, chin rather prominent – everything else ordinary. I have heard people say that I am inclined to be grave, if not dry, and bad-tempered looking. I am hot tempered, I confess, and am easily vexed. My brows are often lowering, I'm afraid. I don't like very_good tempered people – in my imagination they are inclined to be rather childish; they are, I believe, easily imposed upon.

I am of ordinary stature – rather under medium height if anything, & I try to walk straight – I like the military bearing.

My imaginations, I think, differ entirely from those of the everyday, ordinary youth. I like history & geography, any sort of naval or military or political information. I delight in writing stories, composing poetry, etc. I revel in drawing, colouring and painting – in fact I am in my glory, and never happier than when I am surrounded by pictures and works of Art, and have palette & brushes in my hands and canvas before me.

If I had not to depend upon earning my bread by attending an office, I would be constantly engaged in the following pursuits: Painting, designing, sketching (or some other such artistic study), writing stories, poetry, essays, adventures, etc. I used to delight in making and sailing yachts, but it has worn of now. At one time I went in dead for being a soldier – it was many years ago, and I used to love to gather up a regiment of lads about my own age, take command (with their unanimous consent) and "drill" them; perhaps the heroic and military ardour was borne of scarlet uniforms and plumed helmets.

[In Liz's writing] *JT likes cricket but not football*

At another period, a little later, I was really going to join the navy. The thought as to how I should do so, if I would be allowed to do so – if I would be even admitted, never struck me. I think that the "penny horribles" had a lot to do with the piratical sentiment that laid hold of me. I was, only a short time ago, very fond of archery; now I am an Archerist because I work at Archer's. I would not have anyone think that I am an extraordinary sort of an individual, because I see nothing about me that is very brilliant, except perhaps the colours that I use. I have been denounced as a blockhead and a numbskull by one who is now a very intimate friend of mine – namely, my schoolmaster. But then, he is one of that long suffering race of people, and I forgive him freely now – I would deserve the epitaphs at the time, no doubt.

Well, to resume, I would not on any account declare myself any better, altho' I do not think I am any worse than other people. I have a long list of faults, as I have often been told, and as I know – to my sorrow. I am, however, only human.

I am an ardent admirer of nature & all her works. I find grace in all her handwork – I see beauty & sublimity where others, less ardant, see nothing and wonder at my enthusiasm. Pictures and works of Art may be admirably executed & exquisite in colour and delineation – they may enrapture the beholder and leave a lasting impression on the memory – but the pictures and the works of art are only copies from nature's mightier works. What is more soul inspiring than to gaze upon some vast and rugged mountain, which, bathed in hovering blue mists, soft and light, and sparkling bright with every imaginable tint and colour of the rainbow, towers far up and up, beyond the clouds, rearing its lofty craggy peak haughtily over and above everything round about – what more majestic?

Or to sit alone in some elevated and secluded spot, "far from the madding crowd" and busy whirl and swirl of the city, away from the haunts of men and their works, and watch the summer sunset. Bewitchingly beautiful, awe–inspiring, sublime! The great ball of fire slowly descending on his downward course, sinks, in haughty splendour, like a thing of life, in a canopy of crimson and amber, scarlet and purple and gold in magnificent profusion and beautiful harmony. Banish the purple and gold and picture, or try to imagine, or watch – a quiet sunset, with out any gorgeous hues or dazzling brilliancy. A sunset of grey and yellow – nothing more – simple, yet sublime! A pale yellow sky overcast with blue grey clouds, an everyday sunset – watch it, and take heed. Note the everchanging clouds as they dissolve and melt and vanish and take curious shapes, but never for an instant remaining the same as the preceeding – take heed and think of what you have seen.

The sky in all its moods, is well worthy of careful study. On a wild, black, dreary night, when the inky firmament has been overcast with murky clouds, hurrying and scurrying to and fro, before the sudden and fitful gusts of the November wind – on such a night as this have I watched and watched untiring.

And on a serene and tranquil evening, when the deep blue of the sky is sprinkled and studded with innumerable stars, like gold dust, with here and there a nugget of virgin gold, when a full round white moon, or a slender crescent of pale yellow has rode peacefully on high – on such an evening have I watched in wondering admiration.

*   *   *   *   *

I would fain go on and on, but must hurry a little more with the next piece.

The Sea

Stand upon the beach and watch the little wavelets lapping and licking the sand, sparkling in silver – in emerald, and in turquoise, rolling in, head over heels, as it were, in frolicsome glee. Now they are like contented children, happy in their play, delighting in their freedom.

Watch those same waters, when the wind is shrieking and whistling and howling in your ears, on a wild tempestuous night, with a blue-black, cloudy sky overhead; with the vivid and blinding lightning flashing and darting from horizon to horizon, tearing the black masses overhead and revealing beneath the ocean – bleak, grey, green, and capped with boiling white surge; a seething, heaving, boiling mass of foaming waters. Hark at the dull boom of thunder overhead; but it is drowned by the incessant roar of the great green and white breakers as they roll and break in spray upon the beach. List to the thunder and tempest and tumult! See the seething vortex of white specked waters! Is it not thrilling? Is it not supremely grand?

*   *   *   *   *

What is a landscape? A lords mansion built of coloured stones, squared and rounded to a hair's breath, set in a smoothly rolled lawn, with guilded railings and artificial trees planted at regular intervals all around? Bah! Away with <u>man's</u> handiwork; we are now dealing with that of nature.

Smiling corn fields, rich copses, spreading meadows, with here and there a clump of willow trees, a few birches – an oak; a winding river, like a silver riband, twisting and turning and branching off ever and anon. Away in the middle distance let us have some life – some cattle, or sheep, or workers in the hayfield, or the ploughman at work. On the horizon let us put some hills, blue and grey, and bathed in the glory of an evening sunset. The foreground may be rough and rugged and wild. Let there be great brown, mossgrown rocks and ivy clad boulders; brown heath and purple heather and bracken and fern in wild profusion, with a trio of stately pines – all nature – nothing artificial.

Nature must have an Architect – a great Designer – a Creator of infallible skill and unerring judgement. I truly believe in a Supreme Being; therefore, loving His works, I must, of necessity (yet not exactly of necessity, but in duty and admiration) love, and honour Him. People talk of "this weary world", this "wicked world" and denounce "the world, yet it is not "the world" but humanity that is wicked. Our earth is a veritable paradise, a garden of Eden, if we would only use our eyes and see the beauty on every hand.

It is a mystery how some people move and breath and eat and live, like machines, devoid of sentiment or enthusiasm of any kind; how can one see Natures rugged magnificence and forget it, or pass on unmoved and indifferent? Shall I go farther? But I am wandering, I am afraid… Where was I? … Oh! – I am as I said an ardent admirer of nature. I am fond of examining leaves and flowers and shrubs and plants – I am not a botanist, however – I examine them for their grace, their beauty, their symmetry, and their colours. Every succeeding day I take more interest in, I learn more from my surroundings.

Am I blowing my own horn? Am I bragging or boasting?

I sincerely trust not. Anyway I will proceed. By this time I think I have, or ought to have given, an outline, a summary of my character. (I must turn back to see where I am to find my bearings, for I feel at sea.) Well here goes

*   *   *   *   *

(How beautiful & novel-like asterisks look.)

I am rather "sat upon" because I am often in the company of a young lady, who, I am duty bound, compelled to say is one of a thousand.

Listen!

She is 16½ years of age – quite a child I admit, in years, but she can talk sound common sense, (as well as nonsense, of course) and this is a great blessing – rather the exception than the rule among females, and especially among the present-day girls. (It is a natural gift, I think.) Her character is, of course, honourable, pure, and of unblemished reputation. She is thoughtful, kind, sympathetic and sincere, although mischievous and always merry. I am never tired of hearing her talking and laughing. I have never yet seen her frown. She has a sharp tongue. She is frank, and always speaks her mind, which is what I like. This girl does not go into hysterics or into ecstasies, nor yet get into raptures over anything which suits her fancy. She says she likes it, and that is all; her face, or rather her eye speaks the rest. This little maiden, although not remarkably beautiful, has a "comely" face, which anyone might fancy. She would make a good impression anywhere, I am sure, as she did on me from the first.

I consider that the most expressive organ of the human face is, undoubtedly, the eye. It has a language of its own, known only to those who have studied its most interesting dialect. Her eyes are large, and of a colour which in daylight is blue grey and at night appear to be dark. They fairly dance in the light of the street lamps and glow and sparkle like cut & polished stones under the surface of water; they are beautiful eyes undoubtedly. She has a boldly defined nose, a well shaped chin, and mouth to suit her face; the forehead being straight and square. This, I presume, will suffice.

*   *   *   *   *

And now I must state my case? Well, there isn't much to state after all. My friend Andrew S. Hopper introduced and brought us together four or five months ago. Why in face and figure he is not unlike me. Indeed we have been mistaken for each other on many occasions. He has the same dark brown eyes tho' his are of a somewhat lighter shade then mine. The same dark eyebrows and hair, his hair however is more to resemble the brush. He has a bright and intellectual looking face, pleasing and attractive in its openness and frankness. We are not alike in manner or taste or in temperament; he soon makes friends with any of the fair sex, but there I think he is in no way exceptional. (Maybe I am, being awfully uncomfortable in company. I am not so bad now however.)

I think I have known Liz longer than AH, but he spoke to her before me. (Or rather, <u>she</u> spoke to <u>him</u> on the boat.) Liz always admired Andrew. AH was fairly "on" for her, until he brought me into the piece; I spoilt him of her, anyway, and he says now that, at the time he was vexed & even jealous.

Now at the same time I was [Here the writing abruptly changes and there are three pages written by Ada His older sister].

(On this the 18th day of August 1893 Friday night 11-30pm. I your big sister Ada wish, with your permission to address a few motherly remarks to you.

Firstly - I say "Don't be silly, John," I mean as regards your random-shot remarks regarding a certain individual of the female line under my charge. [Ada was Headmistress!]

Remember this- all boys go rather "Off" a bit just at your age, the aforesaid "offness" being caused through the influence of a certain representative of the feminine gender. − − −-

You are too young to be thinking of sweethearts etc. But as I have said before yours is the age of sentiment and in the course of a year or two you will laugh at "What I thought when I was a boy." Perhaps some of those days too, when the "Angel" happens to be some dark haired rosy-cheeked damsel instead of the ethereal one.

And here would my sermon close, O brother John. A.T.

[John resumes] Sister Ada got hold of this book and kindly wrote herein the maternal advice. No doubt she is right – but then neither she or anybody else understands me.

    *   *   *   *   *

[He continues with his story, most of which is in the diary. At the end there is a critique from Liz]

My dear friend

Allow me to say that I think your sister Ada has given you some capital advice. There will be great many changes in the next half dozen years. You will then find you don't want your air castles of today.

Of course when (as Ada predicts) you see your dark eyed Susan and she fulfills my part (& even more) in your life; I shall be sorry to lose your friendship. I shall also be sorry when Andrew finds he has no further need of my company. But if your "black eyed Suzy" and Andrew's "to come yet" desrve both of you I will be content. Till then I suppose I may remain your dearest friend

Lizzie.

[The rest of the notebook is just sketches.]

THE DIARY
Volume 1 1892/3

May, 1892

Mr Dobeson proposes to pay us clerks (Rowat, Stanley & myself) monthly. We reluctantly agree, R. being especially reluctant.

May 7th.

1892 (Not paid today) Rowat gets 10/- sub to begin with. We are quite taken aback at such a sudden change.

June 2nd. 1892

Paid today, £2-12-0 (8/- sub leaves £2-4-0) 12/- per week, about 8 months since we got a rise – of money of course.

June 4th. 1892

Get two days (Whit) holiday. A fine horse belonging Adams, in attempting to leap the fence, dividing Garbutts & Hoppers fields, owing to a heavy "Clog" being fastened to its leg, broke it below the knee. Someone killed it with a pocket knife. Rained hard.

June 16th. 1892 (Thurs.)

Tonight as I was coming from the class, a man aged about 45 with a brown beard, evidently a brewer's cartman, on the opposite side of the road, near the horse trough suddenly stopped for a moment, staggered against the wall, shuffled off & sat down on the kerbstone. He put his head in his hands & blood began to flow out of his mouth in great quantities. Some men ran across, gave him water & sent for Dr Blacklock, but within a few minutes the poor fellow fell back dead, at the moment the Dr arrived. His Wife and little boy were there crying bitterly. His body was removed to 24 Greenfield Terr, Askew Rd, G'shead, only about 700 yards distant. Death appeared in the Chronicle next day. Robert Rose, aged 42. The blood ran down the street like a gutter.

June 27th. 1892

Dunston Hoppings. Cooper's peepshow; John Chambers the Armless wonder; Richardson's Galloping Horses; Murphy's (Walter)

Sea on Land; Murphy's Switch back; Newsom's Roundabout. Cooper's, Mitchell's, Newsom's, Fairhurst's, Smith's & Berryman's Swings, Cocoa nut stands, Aunt Sallies, etc. Good show of people.

July 26th. 1892

Launched Today at Elswick an armed cruiser "Le 9 Juli" (9th. July), 350ft long x 44ft broad, moulded depth 26ft. Displacement 3560 tons, Indicates HP forced draught 23 knots. Armament 4-6" quick firing guns. 8-7" do. 12-3 pdr. guns 12 light guns & 5 torpedo tubes. Splendid launch, Vessel launched by one apprentice who knocked out a chock to soon. Christened when launched. (Sister ship to 25 de Mayo.)

Also launched the Aurora (Formerly torpedo boat engined by Ernest Scott & Co. Close N/cle) 204 ft long, 20 ft broad x 13'4" deep. Displacement 500 tons. speed fed. draught 18½ knots. Aurora has a heavy list to port. Seemingly top heavy. Both vessels for the Argentine republic.

30th. July, 1892, (Sat)

Rolley trip to Lockhalf, Gibside today. Left Chapel at 2 O'clock. Saw Wedding party in two Cabs out of Swalwell. Reached Lockhalf in safety amidst strains of heavenly music from penny trumpets, corncrakes & "Tom & Jerries". Ate & drank & made merry at tea-time. Next proposed to go to the Hall. We could either walk around by the road, a mile and a half, or cross the river thus cut that distance off. But we find to our sorrow that it is impossible to cross without a boat. We get halfway by the stones, but no further. We laboriously roll a huge tree trunk from the bankside, to halfway across, & then with barked shins & skinned knuckles, we stand & then & not until then we find out that we can't get it over the river! Later on some lucky bloke finds a – no not a boat. It was more like a dog kennel or a watchman's cabin on its back. We called it by the name of the

"Corned Beef Tin"! It was half full of water.

Maddock & Jack Thompson propelled it backwards & forwards by means of a rope fastened from one side of the river to the other. They landed four passengers but the rest "Weren't having any", the ladies being especially shy.

The farce ended by Maddock's being set adrift & it was not until he was wet up to the knees that he succeeded in landing again. Enjoyed ourselves immensely during the rest of the day. Got some splendid water from a spring in one of the fields. Sang at the farmer's house (Gave him 10/-) & left in the Rolleys again at 8 o'clock. Reached home in safety.

Total loss – half a knife blade. Cr. to Ned Henderson.

Aug 16th. [1892] (Tues)

Sent sketch of Mother for competition in the "Million".

Aug 30th. [1892]

Heavy showers (Thunder.) Paid today (a day in advance but owing to the petty cash being cleaned out). After making out receipt for £2 14s 0d found that I only had £2 12s 0d to receive, Think Mr D. is taking a rise out of us but no He is only careful is Mr D.

[September] 6th. [1892] (Tues)

Received quite a shock at 6-30 p.m., the news that I had won first prize for the portrait competition. (3 weeks ago since sent off.) Reward 52 Millions (Not money of course, not even paper money, but papers without the money!)

Oct. 3rd. [1892] (Mon.)

Started by 10-20 train for Ayr Scotland.nearly 160 miles from Newcastle on Tyne. Weary ride. Arrived at Ayr at 10 to 5. Wandered about in drizzling rain & slushy streets for half an hour. Got lodgings at Mrs Dickies in town. (Met Mr D. near Central Station he requested me to start again on Saturday!)

[October] 4th. & 5th. [1892]

Took water colour sketches of Old Brig o'Doon, Kirk Alloway & pencil drawings of Burns Statue from model in cottage, also our old guide "John" who recited "Tam o'Shantor to all newcomers to the kirk. Visited Burn's Cottage, Monument, Tam o'Shantor Inn etc. Bought numerous presents.

Oct. 6th. [1892] (Thurs)
Started at 7-40 from Ayr. Reached Dumfries at 11-30 or thereabouts. Visited Burns Mosleum in St Michael's Church, saw house where Burns died, The Globe Tavern, The Observatory, wandered about buying sundry articles and visiting eating houses etc. until 5 when we were rattled along to Newcastle. Lord Tennyson died today at 9-30.

Oct. 7th. [1892] Fri.
On this eventful morning I resolved – alas - to go to N/cle for some canvases. Met Mr D. on boat landing!
Wished me to come THAT AFTERNOON! He had a lot of invoices etc. to make out, of course & books to post up etc. etc. I went to N/cle nevertheless and got a canvas 18x12″. Started work this afternoon.

27th. October. 1892
Thurs. Heavy wind. Little warmer.
Our Epitaph (Office)
Oh! for a fire to warm our frozen limbs!
To lighten up our dreary office wings.
A single cinder would be more to us;
Then all the pens and rulers of the universe.
But e'en so small a boon is stern denied.
We can but only hope,
Though oft have sighed. J.T.

November 27th. 1892 (Sunday)
I am 17 today. A Great day in the annuls of the nation. But the glorious anniversary passed "Unwept, unhonoured & unsung!" It is just the way of the world. Great men are of no consequence now a days.

December 21st. [1892] (Wed)
School Concert tonight. Began at 7. Crowded House (School). Several girls sang & one or two recited, but the centre of attraction was the playing of the trial scene from "The Merchant Of Venice" in which the following celebrated characters took part.

Portia (Lily Taylor)	Antonio (Ben Arkless)
Shylock (Willie Tatton)	Bassanio (Ernest Gladstone)
The Duke (Charlie Lucas)	Gratiano (Tom Brown)

The play was carried of very successfully. Portia acted like Ellen Terry, but Shylock SCARCELY came up to Henry Irving. He was very stiff & dropped about like a piece of wood. The Duke appeared to be very composed too, and talked to the Jew in a very sensible manner.

[December] 25th. Sun [1892]

Carol Singers sung "Christians Awake" & another rattling hymn. Got up at 11-10 a.m. in time for dinner. Goose, Rabbit & Plum Pudding at 1-30. Everything passed off very quietly not even a row.

January 1893. 1st. (Sunday)

The Old year went out with a bang from various quarters. It was long after two this morning when the inmates of no 23 A. St. retired for repose, after being entertained for some considerable time by Messrs. Noble, Maddock, Golightly & etc. Got up at about eleven O'clock, but could scarcely walk for my sprained foot. Was off school in the afternoon too. All our people had tea at Ravensworth Road & I limped up at my best pace & joined them.

Feb. 21st. (Tues.) [1893]

Began to colour "Discobolus" tonight & was so enraptured in it that I did not take perspective. Paid 5/- for new session.

Feb. 22nd. [1893] (Wed)

Sketched four figures schoolboys singing & entitled it "Harmony" but it is questionable whether harmony would be raised from such a quartette.

March 9th. 1893. (Thurs)

Worked three hours overtime tonight painting Dunston Engine Works name on a 26 ft Boiler. Just fancy! 26 feet of 18 "x 2" thick letters, in a gale of wind up a rickety ladder.

[March]10th. [1893] Friday

Received some severe criticisms from practical men! about the letters on the boiler. A second two hours finished'em off tonight. (Two classes missed)

[March] 15th. [1893]

Ordered a 45 x 32 canvas. I have resolved to hazard a large figure study entitled "The Spy".

[March] 19th. Sunday [1893]

Tonight as AH & I went up the lane from the Chapel, Misses P &

T passed & asked him something, while I waited patiently in the background. & I began for the first time to talk to them

26th. March [1893] (Palm Sunday)

No Sunday school, Mr Ogden preached at night. Was better introduced to Miss Lizzie Pugmyre much to my satisfaction.

30th. March [1893] Thurs.

Rec. £3/3/- wages less 5/- sub & only 4/- for lettering boiler, never more! Mr D. is rapidly changing as regards benevolence. (To have 4 days)

2nd. April [1893] Sunday

Tonight I had the audacity to set a Lady home!

Holiday Tues. 4th. April [1893]

Total hours at picture about 36. Went to Miss Henderson's Kinderspiel at seven. Had I only known that this was the dear girls (Miss P.) birthday of sixteen!

April 9th. [1893]

Set Miss Pugmyre home for second Sunday night.

April 25th. [1893] Tues

Met Mr Johnson Hedley tonight & had a talk with him. He is going to write me particulars about his sketching club which I am thinking of joining.

May 2nd. [1893] Tues

D.E.Works almost laid in for a few days whilst the rivitters were mending boiler. Catastrophe today. One of the boiler tubes burst and unluckily one of the heaters happened to be passing at the critical moment. The result was disastrous. He was drenched with filth and dirty water from head to foot. Paid £3-3-0 less 5/- = £2-18-0 today for salary due 30th. April.

May 4th. [1893] (Thurs)

Saw Miss P up at the 4 Lane ends tonight & Miss. Lucas so I brought them home again.

May 5th. [1893] Fri.

Wrote a P/c to Mr Hedley. Am surprised at his silence after promising to write.

May 10th. [1893] Wed.

Arrived at the School of Art at 7 and began at once with the

Modelling. Examiner Major Wolner. (Bro of an R.A ? Can? .) At half time the gallant Major had a look round & most highly complimented my model. Said he "It looks as if it had been well licked! I thought from that, that I need expect no mercy however I was somewhat reassured a little later. [Two lines erased.]

May 16th. [1893]

Saw Mr Johnson Hedley today. Wants some sketches. Did an oil sketch of Thomas snr.

May 19th. [1893] Friday.

Went for a walk with Andrew tonight and met Miss P. herself. She was very kind and looked exceedingly happy. She and Miss T are going to the Art Gallery tomorrow. (19¹/₂ hrs. at Spy) (Showery) Tom took the sketches to Mr Hedley tonight & he was delighted at my successful efforts.

June 5th. [1893] (Mon)

Altered the sky in "The Spy" into a sunset. 2/- from Ed. 12/- total. Mr. Hedley (N.C. Sketching club) did not write. Went per 6-30 boat and after an hour & halves hunt found out the rooms of the club at No. 6 Ridley Place, Northumberland St. N/cle. I was introduced by Mr. Hedley to the other members numbering about fourteen, & warmly received. Was elected a member unanimously; & congratulated by Mr. Hedley the President, Mr Fisher & Mr Ventress Vice-presidents, & by the Sectry. Mr. McKendrick.

It was after ten when the committee meeting broke up, & 10-45 when I got home tonight. I must send 7/6 to Mr Munro or Mr, McK. as soon as possible. Its nothing but spending now. All my pocket money & twice as much vanishes with alarming rapidity, & it is as much as I can do to keep out of debt. Oh! that I had a banking account or a rich uncle!

[June]12th. [1893] Monday

Time 10-40 p.m. Hurrah! Ada has been appointed Head Mistress Infant Board School. Best news we've heard for many a week!

[June] 16th. [1893] (Fri.)

(Alfred Leathard Taylor born at 1 this morning. Another calamity)

SOLILOQUY! Lizzie is now constantly with Miss. Jenny T. I don't think she gets any good from Her. Anyway I scarcely have a chance of seeing L. by herself. Jenny seems to stick to her, & she to Jenny like glue. I wouldn't for the world poison L's mind against Jenny for they have been friends so long. I always think it strange that a girl like Liz. should associate with one of Jenn's nature. They are entirely different – or were a very short time ago. Now however Liz is slowly tho. certainly losing her quiet & modest ways. Still I like her now (I confess it) more then ever. She is very free & chatty now. I hope no harm will come of her associations with Jenny. Jenny has said some rather insulting things about me, but when I am in her company she is one of the kindest of girls. I now sum up with my verdict of Miss. L.P. She is one of the most affectionate of her sex. She can talk common sense, (as well as nonsense) when it suits her to do so. & that is one great blessing. Most of girls talk about the most ridiculous things but Liz as I have said, just suits me for talking.(She has a sharp tongue nevertheless.) She is polite, interesting &–&–& er Lovable! (I am afraid this is foolish but it is the impression I get just now. Anyone who reads this unknown to me except after my coffin has left the house, is a confounded sneak, ladies not included though.

Well now, when I am in the mood I will tell what L. is dressed in. She looks smart indeed in dark crimson (She doesn't call it crimson– in her eyes it is ruby col'd or something of the sort.) with a swiss belt. I am always admiring this swiss belt, where she keeps her watch, which article by the way gains 5 minutes every day & causes the owner, when wanting to know the time of day, considerable trouble. The Swiss belt is laced at the front, the ends of the aforementioned laces hanging below in a neat rose knot.

Her Hats: One a brown Tam o'shanter sort of article kept on the head by means of a cruel looking lance, stuck through the head has only recently been discarded. Another, gone from sight, black, perforated, riddle like straw & I forget what else. The present weekday one is dark brown straw, strictly geometrical in shape, with dark yell. ochre (I call the colour. I believe in the female world it is dubbed "Old Gold" or something similar & outlandish) Ribbon in bits here & there.

The other Hat is also straw, light cream colour (to use a lady's words) more artistic looking with a piece looped up at the back &

some sort of ribbon etc.
embellishing it. I'll take more
notice next time I see these
articles of apparel. She wears shoes,
and that will finish that item and
conclude the critique. I might say
something more about this young
lady later on perhaps. I could fill a
volume in her praise. I hope I
shall never alter my
opinion of her.

Lizzie is glad that Ada
is to be Mistress of the
Infants School, so is Misses
Jenny Lucas & Satchwell, as
well as Miss Singer.

Miss Hunter professes to be
pleased But–

June 17th. [1893]
We are to have only two days Holiday! (Wed & Thurs) Shameful!
Outrageous ! ! ! Nothing special for Mon & Tues. either & Mr. D.
away at Glasgow! ! ! I'll say no more or my feelings may overcome me

19th. June [1893] Mon.
Came to office this morning after 1½ hours painting and 20 mins
cycling with a bronzed and polished face & heavy heart. – How can
anybody work during a general holiday. Done at 4-30.

[June] 20th. [1893] (Tues.).
Touched up the big picture again & then at night went for my as
per usual nightly stroll.The Picture I will here describe. This is the
impression that I have attempted to convey to the spectator. The
following is what I would like the thing to be.

The scene represents the interior of a fashionable walnut panelled
room (which shows unmistakable signs of confusion) at the time of
the 1870–3 Franco German War. It is nightfall, the pale yellow eastern
sky seen through a broad window on the right is rapidly being
overcast with blue grey clouds hovering over the roofs and spires of

buildings away in the blue distance, & indications of a storm are apparent, by the unearthly sort of light which pervades the room.

There are five figures: the principal who first attracts attention is a young french soldier – The prisoner of war (La Prisonare du Guerre) who stands near the centre of the picture, defiant, fearless and proudly erect with scornful contempt written in his handsome face, yet his white clenched hands & pale features show that he is fully alive to the extreme gravity of his awful situation. Death – the inevitable doom – is to him something more then mere glory – a hideous reality. At the opposite end of the crimson covered table, laid for desert sits the General before whom the culprit has been brought, and by his chair stands his subordinate officer – a grave old campaigner with a grey beard, who seems to have a soft heart for the young man before him as he glances first from the prisoner to the grim old general, trying to fathom his thoughts, or expecting to see some shade of pity relax the iron features. The German pipe in the hand of the commander is what relieves and softens the frown on his face, & the surroundings tend to take away the sternest of the judges. Behind the prisoner is guarded by a couple of Prussian soldiers standing out grimly against the dark red drapery of the back-ground. The soldiers may be summed up with as follows:- The one young, unused to the ghastly horrors of warfare pitying, the other, a bronzed & bearded veteran looking utterly unconcerned & in another direction. A large dog in the fore- ground is in the act of rising from one of the rugs covering the polished floor & is eyeing the bluecoated frank suspiciously from under his shaggy eyebrows. The trio of figures on either side of the table are compact in harmony with the Rembrandt like background, the General, his friend, & the dog agreeing with the French and the two Prussian soldiers, without being distasteful to the eye the colouring of the whole is brilliant, yet by no means crude or showy.

What shall be the title of this masterpiece? I have thought of "The Spy", "The Courtmartial", "The Prisoner of War" & "Awaiting Sentence."

I do like the face of the french soldier which is nicely coloured ditto with left hand. The pose is good. The face of the Colonel is well done – bronzed. The books lying near the dog & the dog itself are I think capital. The Tablecloth, the mantleshelf & its surroundings, Mr. Ogden said were splendid. The pictures on the wall I like. The cornice part of the ceiling & the candelabra are very good.

[June] 21st. [1893] Wed.

I saw Them tonight. I asked Liz. if she had any notion of going to Cullercoats, but she does not care for the seaside – (neither do I).

[June] 22nd. [1893] (Thurs)

Went down to Cullercoats & stayed there all day. Took 2¹/₂ hours to go down & 4! to come back. Never shall I forget that eventful voyage. It began to rain, there was no cover for the deck of the passenger boat & I had to stand crushed and miserable for what seemed many years of prolonged torture. Gave up my seat for ladies both ways, (There's generosity for you!) Got back home safe & sound (?) at 9-30. Did not go to the moor this year. Only passable I hear.

June 23rd. [1893] (Fri.)

An Awful naval disaster occurred off Tripoli (Syrian coast). Whilst manoeuvring the "Camperdown" rammed the "Victoria" & ripped up her starboard side causing her to sink within 13 minutes, with Admiral Tryon & 430 officers & men. The "Victoria" was built at Elswick & launched in April 1887. There must have been mismanagement somewhere I think. Court Martial to be held at Portsmouth.

June 24th. [1893] (Sat)

Went to Low Fell this afternoon, to sketch with S. of Art chaps but I never saw one of them. The rain greatly aided my efforts to make a sketch. I got back home somewhat uncomfortable & damp about five. No lesson at Mr. Ogden's today, but I went up later on for some colour & had a chat with him.

June 26th. [1893] Mon

Looked uncompromising this morning but it was a splendid day & quite fair at night when the fun began at the Hoppings. There were plenty of people but not much to see. The switchback carriages & galloping horse roundabout took the monopoly. The four of us (Misses P.& T. AH & yours truly) knocked a bit about together in the cars etc. It was eleven o'clock (!) when Lizzie's "Matergrande" came in search of the little dear, but she did not scold her much.

[June] 27th. [1893] (Tues.)

A beautiful day but breezy, went to Hoppings tonight again. Not quite such a crush as last night, but the rain which fell rather heavily at one time made up for last nights squirting. Liz allowed until 11-15 tonight. We three (AH is working again poor wretch!) were in the cars again.

June 28th. [1893] (Wed)

Mr J. Hedley came to our house tonight & examined my picture. He gave me many useful hints & good suggestions by which I might improve it, and thought it was a very bold start for me to make. I did not do much work tonight. The sunsets are beautiful now I must get some outside sketching done these nights. Rained tonight so I sought shelter under Mr Hall's hospitable roof.

[June] 30th. [1893] (Fri.)

I got rather a fright this morning. I noticed a young lady emerging from the precincts of No. 14 Athol Street. She was I discovered one whom I knew, but alas! instead of seeing the usual flow of golden streamers over her shoulders, I beheld the luxurious wealth rolled up in a knot upon the top of the head! What a change! I hope to goodness she isn't going to begin putting up her hair like that already. It makes a girl look staid at once.

Another beautiful day. Paid to-night £3-3-0, less 15/- for subs. I have not yet got that 10/- due to me from

Mr. Boldon, promised for last Sat. Of course it will be all right. I'll go over for it tonight. (later, no I forgot) Rather hazy tonight but I went "for nightly stroll". Came down with Miss P. & Miss Jenny Satchwell. The former lady does not intend to wear her hair up. "Not likely" she is right there! She & Miss T are going to Shields tomorrow. I am going to Seaton Sluice with Mr. Hedley. Lizzie knew nothing about the Sunday school trip next Thurs. until I enlightened her on the point & says she does not think Miss T. will be able to get, in which case she will not go. We shall see.

[July] 3rd. [1893] (Mon)

Did a sketch for Sk. Club tonight & went to N/c per 7-30 boat. Good assembly in spite of dull weather. I was introduced to Mr Wm. Wilde. Came over to Gh'd with Miss Swift & Mr Wilde & got home at 10-30 about. Miss Swift gave me some well meant advice tonight by which I might profit when sketching. I Took it all in but kept quiet. I like advice from competent authorities or from one who is better at the art then myself.

[July] 4th. [1893] (Tues)

I had a walk tonight. Met Misses P. & T. in coming down. Liz was in by 9-25 tonight! Good girl!

[July] 5th. [1893] Wed.

Time 3-35 p.m. Place D. E. Works Office,

Characters Mr. D., Rowat, Stan, Ismay & myself. (Tomorrow a general Holiday Royal Wedding). Mr. D. "Eer-ah-come tomorrow morning –" (Exit) The others myself included join in the doleful dirge and swear our minds to our hearts content. Did the walk once more tonight. But there is really nothing outrageous in going with a girl, so long as she is of unassailable honour. But then there are always three! of us. What harm can there be in the walks. Liz got in tonight at 10 punctual. The clock was striking as she entered, in fact she informed me. Rather a fine day.

1893 July 6th. (Thurs)

Royal Wedding day. General Holiday.Splendid weather now. I did not feel supremely happy this morning as I wended my weary way Archerwards. But it was not to be so bad after all, we got away at 10-30. Went home of course, & was occupied in brightening the polished work of bicycle for 3½ hours, until two o'clock! Well I got my dinner, packed up colour box and sketch block, mounted my bi-wheeler & went up the lane for a sketch. Alas for the sketches I got! Before you arrive at the 4 Lane Ends there is built a seat, o'ershaded by a gnarled Oak tree! Quite a romantic looking spot! A veritable novel trysting place. The tree is hollow to receive the love letters too. Well I was about to pass the fatal spot when I looked & behold I saw three familiar forms, two especially familiar, and one of the two even more especially familiar. The last mentioned lady in her brown and yellow hat & great brown cloak, Blue dress, low shoes, watch chain, flowers etc. looking particularly nice. How could I pass?

Sketching was forgotten. Dreams of delicate olive greens & verdant browns faded into oblivion & vanished at the sight I now saw; prussian blues & purple madders begone! I alighted gracefully enough, luckily on my feet, ran the wheeler into the pathway & sat down beside them. (By the way I think we monopolise that seat now. During the hours we sat there numbers of persons came panting up to the seat (the mercy seat I might call it) people tired out, who seemed to have made a last effort to reach the place where they might rest their weary selves–alas! they toiled in vain & to no purpose, only to find the seat filled up! But this life is made up of disappointments.!) Well to return. We sat there for a jolly long time, during which I drew portraits of Liz and Miss Satchwell.

Miss Tatten decamped some time before this with my sister Minnie, who rather frightened her I think, by saying that she would let Mrs. Tatten know. At four o'clock we came down again. Liz & Jen S. went up later on to Whickham (Mr Bourn's) to get some flowers. On their return I intercepted the pair. We hied to that everlasting seat, (It was about 9 o'clock now) & there I got a flower from Liz – a "Maidens blush" Rose. Now I never put in my buttonhole a flower of very brilliant colour & the diameter of the same must not exceed ½ of an inch: this rose was a pretty pale pink & might have been nearly an inch, but I put it in all the same; how could I do otherwise? Besides it was such a little beauty–like the donor herself. I then showed her the photo sketch I had finished from the school group. Apparently she admired it. Later Liz & Jen showed it to the "Grandmater" & she pronounced a very favourable judgement. To return to the 9 o'clock scene at the seat– well I return when there is nothing more to say. Liz & Jenny S. left for home & I went up again. Somehow I can't think of going home now when out at night before ten. I had scarcely been left alone a quarter of an hour – I was sitting on the railings writing in this very diary–when what should I hear but the merry chatterbox voice of "The little dear", who with her inseparable consort in tow, suddenly came in sight. Of course I was in duty bound, compelled to accompany them to the "Four lane ends" & back home again. Liz would fain have stayed later than 10 to see the gorgeous display of fireworks (On the occasion of Prince George's Marriage) but as she said a stately figure in a white apron, tall, stern, & commanding, grim & unrelenting loomed in her mind's eye.

Her Grandmaters word was law. She & Jen skipped up to no. 14. However I saw her a little later on the quay, eating something, & with a shawl wrapped around her shoulders (careful girl). We watched for a few minutes but the display which might have been brilliant enough did not exactly act up to the point now. (Perhaps Liz was afraid her Grandmater would come to seek her, for she had slipped out whilst that lady was engaged in conversation with a neighbour) & she got back by about 10-20. At 10-20 I shook hands for the third time and left her alone with her glory (& her Grandmater).

[July] 8th. [1893] (Sat).

Today I wrote the following note to Liz who is ill; "Dear Girl; Kindly allow me to convey to you my deepest sympathy for your indisposition. Sincerely trusting that you will soon be well again. I beg to remain your earnest friend etc. I hope she does not think me impertinent. Miss Jenny T. kindly delivered the note.

[July] 10th. [1893] (Mon)

Ada began to teach for a fortnight at Winlaten Schools to oblige Miss Atkinson. Ada begins at the Board schools on 1 st August. I went for a walk tonight, but did not see Lizzie. Saw Miss T. at Dun Cow, who said that the little dear was nursing her Grandmater who is ill. She must be like a ministering angel. Jen said that she was not at all vexed with my note

Friday [July] 14th .1893]
This afternoon I finished Lizzie's photo. I went up to the meeting at Gateshead Sch. of Art & showed my portrait for a sketch. I was pleased by the way they praised it. (I have portrait sketching on the brain now, Mr Rowatt says that I have something else there, namely Love!) What foolish ideas some people get into their heads. I am in Love! Doesn't it sound nice & romantic– Oh yes! Rowat says I will commence the shooting & suicide business shortly– the impertinence of such people is simply disgusting!

I met or rather went to meet the "Two fair maids", we met on the doorstep almost of Mrs. T's & I showed them the finished photo. "Oh! Its Grand! Lizzie said a dozen times over, but the words were full of meaning. She was really delighted, so was Jenny (Miss T) who said it was a splendid likeness. "Oh! Its Grand! "cried the "Dear Girl " again & again and I was never more satisfied or happier. Liz's birthday is on April 4th. I must remember it, I have a long-time to wait.

By Jove it is 12-20 at night or rather Sat morning when I am writing all this rubbish. I'll have another look at the little girls happy face & then upward ho! for the night!

The likeness is good indeed.

Sat 15th. July [1893]
I had to run off to the boat rather hastily this morning at 9-30, as Mr. Rowat had not arrived with the Black bag (Wages) & when I arrived, Rowat had been there already ,got the money after all, and walked up. I liked the sail all the same of course. At seven-30 I went up the lane for a walk. Sat beside Misses Wheatley & Satchwell for some time and then THEY came up. Did I go with them? Why

certainly I did. It was rather late so we went down. I gave Liz her photo & she was in the seventh heaven of delight.

23rd. [July] Sun. [1893]

Saw Liz this afternoon after S.school. She went to Miss T's for tea. The two sat in the pew before us tonight & giggled & laughed the whole of the time. If Misses T. & P. behave in such a way next Sunday night (When we have to give our Missionary addresses) as they did tonight, I shall certainly break down. We had only talked for a few minutes when Liz's Matergrande came to seek Willie. (Lizzie's little brother. By the way she has other two brothers– Harry age 14 & George about 19, I think. The latter she is always talking about!) When the old lady had vanished I produced a long scroll & after some palaver began to read in a solemn tone. "I know a Maid – a Maid so fair, with laughing eyes of colour rare; that sparkle bright in liquid blue and ever dance with mischief new, etc. etc. After numerous interruptions I at length drew towards the close which runs thusly. "She's like an Angel from above, And this is she the Girl I Lo___! I never finished the sentence for the paper was snatched from my hand & crumpled up in Miss Tatten's. I became really frightened for Liz had turned her back & walked away saying a cold "Good night". I looked (somewhat appealingly I believe) though rather indignantly at Miss T. She slowly unrolled the scroll and smoothly folded it up saying "For shame John Taylor". Liz gurgled out "Tear it up". I half fancied that Liz had fairly become mad with me. For sometime we hold a desultory sort of random shot conversation, during which the little girl gradually drew nearer.

Then I came in hot for it. I was denounced, unanimously as being "Cracked." Said complimentary Miss. T. "John! I never thought you were so far gone as all that" Now I am set down as being all gone. Liz again advised Jen to tear the poetry into pieces; but Jen understood the way in which the other dear said it and refrained. I knew then that Liz really was shamming. I know now that she actually, really & certainly liked it. Liz got home by 10 past 10 & her M.grande was rather waxy in consequence.

July 24th. (Monday) [1893]

Wesleyan Trip today. I got up at 6-30 & went down to the landing at 8-30. The trip boat had not gone. I would have been earlier to get the tickets but Liz had told me that her GrandPater was going down, so that I could not very well see what else to do. I found the three (viz Liz. & her G-pater & Miss. S.) GrandPater got out at Dun St. landing, and we were happy then. We had a beautiful sail down the river & arrived at the Tynemouth pier at about 9-45. We got out & had a walk first down the rocks. We then went into the town & down, on to the sands, just before the Dunston people (Wesleyans) among whom were a lot of Archer's apprentices.

On the sands we sought out a secluded spot where we amused ourselves, until nearly 12-30 with burying each other in sand, combing our hairs, brushing up, destroying sandwiches & with other varied & trivial amusements too numerous to mention singly. It was about 1 o'clock when we went into some cocoa rooms, had some tea & sandwiches & afterwards a wash & brush up. We then went into the railway station, after talking a bit to Miss Black whom we met. Next we visited Voses toffee shop, then went onto the banks besides the Collingwood monument where we enjoyed ourselves until nearly five. We watched the fishing fleet go out, told stories, carved our names on the seat, gathered flowers from over the brink of the awful precipices etc. & many more things, when we decided to have a look round the town. We got something to eat on the boat & then embarked on the Felling Trip boat to Felling. We had all to stand for the best part of the journey. At Jarrow there was a sudden gust of wind & rain, which quickly increased into a perfect deluging torrent of water. In a few minutes we were all wet. The people in the forepart of the boat made a rush for the covering abaft the funnel & we were crushed out. Liz however managed to squeeze herself into a seat & Jen sat on her knee. I stood before them with my back to the storm. I was soon drenched & cold. The rain continued for about 20 minutes without intermission; then the sun shone brilliantly & there was a beautiful sunset.

We arrived at Gateshead Boatlanding at ? to 9, & walked down Gateshead. At the Chapel we saw Jenny (Miss T.) (Miss.S. had left us then) We three talked until about twenty to ten when as a natural consequence we parted.

1/- from Mater for lunch.

George (Lizzie's brother) referring to the question asked by Jenny, as to whether Liz. had enjoyed herself, remarked: "Why aye; wasn't she sure to be happy:- the first time out with her husband!" .

July 25th. (Tues). [1893]

Mr. Johnson Hedley called tonight. I was busy with a small canvas, He greatly admired the big picture again & suggested a few more little improvements by which I hope to profit. He thinks it quite a handsome picture & a capital success.

July 27th. (Thurs) [1893]

Mr. Rowat landed this morning the worse for drink, but it wore of by night. Saw Mr. Hepple who promised to come up to our house, tomorrow night at 5-30 to see my big canvas. Walked down, part of the way, with two friends, when I came to the seat and found the two. Certainly I said Goodnight" to the gentlemen and sat down beside them. We three came down together, and Liz got home by 10 o'clock.

July 28th. (Fri) [1893]

I had expected Mr Wilson Hepple tonight by the 5-30 boat, but he did not arrive until half past six when I showed him all my sketches and pictures. He admired the stag picture (done at Mr Ogden's). He thought the figure picture too great a subject for me to attempt (of course it was) but on the whole "Very Good". He suggested one or two little improvements. We went for a jolly long walk tonight.

Now I am going to make a confession. (I don't see any harm or anything outrageous in it but strangers might.) This is it:

By this time I beg to say that I am extremely fond of Miss. L. P. & I hope, trust, expect, (nay truly believe!) that she likes me! I hope I am not denounced, by this time, as being mad when I am writing this. The house has retired, it is 5 past 12 on Saturday morning, and I am alone except for the cat, the flies and the back beetles, yet I am quite sane!

July 29th. (Sat) [1893]

This is Ada's birthday. The girl is 20 today. A full fledged mistress of a large infants school. The very idea of a girl like Aada Taaylor taking the place of a person like Miss Henderson!! It is too much!

July 30th. (Sun.) [1893]

Mr Ogden preached at chapel this morning. Ada had a birthday party at tea time. The great address came off tonight. At six I went down to the vestry with Mr Jack Noble. Andrew S. H. (junior) gave his address first. His first words in giving out the hymn no. 948 were very faint indeed. As his speech went on he got better. He was on only about six or seven minutes. He got on well & his address was exceedingly good though not very deep. The last address, given by Mr A. T. Hopper (senior) was rather violent & more emphatic then pointed. Both of these addresses were composed mainly of "Surface matter" (I mean to say that they were not exactly pointed or deep enough. This is my candid opinion without being in any way prejudiced. I got on all right with mine; it was not so bad after all.) I went on for 22 minutes. There was a very good attendance, although it rained & all were exceedingly attentive. The other two addresses were very interesting. Collection: £1-19-0$^1/_2$

I was congratulated by four or five ladies and gentlemen and felt somewhat stuck up. By the way, the trio (Misses P., T. and S.) came in rather late and took up their quarters in one of the long centre pews. But they kept pretty quiet.) Lizzie's Matergrand is still ill. However we met the dear girl coming up (lower down then Miss T's door) and we went down again together.

July 31st. (Mon.) [1893]

Liz was talking to Lillie today about the speeches last night. She (Liz) said the same about mine to Lillie as she said to me last night,

WALKING THE LANES WITH LIZ

namely that she did not care so much for mine as she did for Andrew's. I like to hear anybody praise up AH for he is a really worthy fellow. However she had no right to run me down in the eyes of others. She thought that Andrew had a better style of delivery then me. I think though that I said mine best and that my speech was first by a long chalk. I like her cheek however. She is very independent I see now. Ada takes charge of the Infant school tomorrow. A lady remarked to Miss T. the other day that I was being made a sandwich of.

August 1st. (Tues.) [1893]

After tea I went up with painting paraphernalia to the four lane ends. It was too wet last night. Before I had pitched my easel, I had about ten spectators, the number rapidly increasing, amounting in time to over a score. Mr. Hepple was with me for a long time. Misses P. and S. passed when I was about finished with my night spell. I packed up at 9, after 2 hours work.

August 3 rd (Thurs.) [1893]

Oh, the rain! Simply lovely!! So beautiful was it that I put on that hateful greatcoat of mine!!! I felt rather warm when I arrived at the D. E. Works. Rowat did not arrive until 10-30. What awful stuff "stock taking" is. Everybody is heartily sick of it. We are now looking forward to holidays. Mr D. travels from someplace down the water to work now. Stan is to have his holiday first. I went to Teams tonight to be shorn (at the advice of Miss. P. I may say!) of some of my superfluous wool, i.e. hair. (It is a queer thing, and the hair must be long, when a girl has to tell a chap about it).

August 9th. (Wed.) [1893]

Fair weather, but very hot. I saw Liz tonight, up beside Peacock's house, alone! Jen can't get out at nights just now. Her Pater is in a bad mood just now. We got home by 10 to 10.

August 17th.(Thurs.) [1893]

Got a post card this morning from Mr White saying that the result of the exams would be in the "Chronicle" tonight. I have passed first in elemtry, shading, but only second Clay modelling. Of course perspective – passing was out of the question. The work that I sent up to Kensington must not have been accepted. Mr White (headmaster) said that he should be disappointed (but I had not to be) if I did not get a first class certificate for the sepia drawing of "Discobolus" – well I suppose I can't make a better of it but truly I am grieved and sorely disappointed. I met Liz & Miss S. coming down and also did likewise. We saw Miss. T. and her cousin; and then, why keep repeating?

August 18th. (Fri.). [1893]

Tonight as I was writing this Ada got hold of another book of mine in which I write daily thoughts, sundries and such like, and after reading all through (Including the poetry "I Know a Maid") wrote the following: "On this the 18th. day of August 1893 Friday night 11-30 p.m. I your big sister Ada wish with your permission to address a few motherly remarks to you. Firstly I say 'Don't be silly John' I mean as regards your random shot remarks regarding a certain little individual of the female line, under my charge. (Ada is Liz's Mistress now you know) Remember this, all boys go off (!) a bit, just at your age, the aforesaid offness being caused thro' the influence of a certain representative of the feminine gender.

I wish to make a protest against that libel you attach to 'Our' (The females of our household, so I presume) set. I mean the charge of giving you out as being 'Mad daft, soft, demented etc.' Believe me dear brother, if such has been said –though it does sound rather TOO– it has been said with the sole object of doing you good. You are too young to be thinking of sweethearts etc., but as I have said before, yours is the age of sentiment, & in a year or two you will laugh at 'what I thought when I was a boy', perhaps some of these days too when the 'Angel' happens to be some dark haired rosy cheeked damsel instead of the ethereal one.

And here would my sermon close. Oh, brother John! A. T."

I COLLAPSE.

I did not ask Ada to read the book; far from wishing her to do so. Yet I did not prevent her. (Of course I could altho' she thinks I could not.) She read it without the quiver of a muscle, her face was, all the while immovable as that of a redman–

What am I to think of the criticism! Strange to say, wonderful to relate! I too was unmoved – I saw my "big" (she is a few inches less than me, I think) sister writing in the book (with my permission) but I thought she was busy with something relating to the Character of

Miss. P. Now when I come to think soberly of what I have set down in writing, I don't wonder at anyone thinking me demented. It is all bosh to any ordinary being, what I have written – only A.Hopper understands me and what I write. In him I have found a confidant. He knows me and he knows Liz perfectly, therefore he can see through the writing – read between the lines, as it were. I am very grateful for Ada's practical and "motherly" advice. She is quite right (altho' bye the bye, she is "dead on" herself, with a certain male person by name Wm. Maddock esq., organist, clerk, etc. etc., residing both at Gateshead & Dunston).

August 24th. (Thurs.) [1893]

Rained a bit today & rather chilly at night. P/c from N/Cle Sketching club stating that there will be a meeting on the Mon night first (last Mon in Aug instead of the first) and

that the exhibition will be on from Oct. 2nd. to 31st. I don't know I'm sure whether to lug that great picture over again. I might get some useful hints. I went out for a long spin on wheels, Fernacres Way tonight. Got back at 7-30. I went up the lane for a walk. There was a beautiful moon, but the light in the eastern sky suddenly revealed to me as I reached the four lane ends, two female figures perched aloft on the railings & standing out in bold relief against the pearly green & brilliant red of the sky. I said Good evening to Misses P. and S. We talked a bit and then came down. We parted

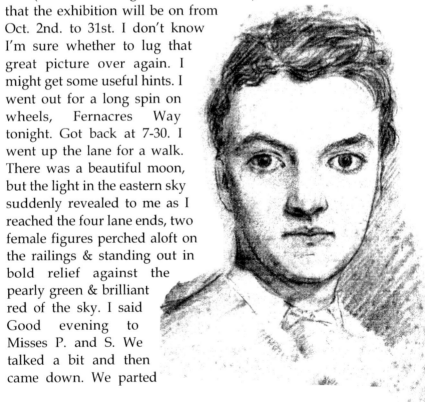

with Jen at the foot of Spoor Street.

Dear me ! What strange things we talk about now! Other people's dress, looks, peculiarities, manners, habits, virtues and vices!! I had got a letter from AH this afternoon and when I told Liz, she was anxious to see it. When I got home tonight I sketched my own portrait again – was on $1^3/_4$ hours until the "wee sma' hours" of Friday morning when brother Ned came in.

This reminds me: Liz said tonight that I dressed better then Ed! (Silly girl!) That she liked my dark blue suit!! That – but I won't go further. It is too much like flattery which I don't like or rather must not like. Girls like to be flattered I know by this time.

August 27th. (Sun): [1893]

I got up at 10-30 this morning! I came to Chapel, I got into the porch, I looked in; I saw every seat filled (except one in which sat ___.) However I went in; the back seat was not filled but I was not going to sit beside a lot of roughs and back sliders, what was I to do? My mind was soon made up. I went into the aforesaid seat; I was now next to __ whom? __ who indeed __ but Misses P. and T! Sitting beside 'em!!! SHE spoke!! The two were quieter in chapel tonight then usual, as a natural consequence of my being beside them.

August 28 th (Mon.) [1893]

I went down in the 6-30 boat with the big picture and some smaller sketches to the Sk: Club. Got a lad to carry the thing to Northumberland St. I arrived at 7-00 and Mr. McKendrick at 7-15. There were some new members there tonight – that is, new to me. Mr S. J. Wilde was there and with him I came over from Newcastle to Gateshead. My picture was thought very good. Some of the members thought it excellent, others pointed out weak places, by which I might profit by rectifying. All agreed that it was a great undertaking for one so young. I got home at 10-45. The exhibition of pictures Oct. 2nd. to 31st. Expect about 100 pictures.

Conversazione on Oct. 2nd. and opening. Mr J. Hedley was not there tonight.

August 31st. (Thurs.) [1893]

I met a lady on the way – one with whom I am slightly acquainted with viz. Miss Liz. P. We went up a bit farther together, but soon after returned. Liz. likes to stand at the old corner, talking to me better than walking and speaking; besides the lane is so much "worn" so common - now. Well we came down & took up our usual position for the night.

We were attracted, however, by the brilliantly glaring rays from the search lights of the Japanese warship at Elswick and went over to the railway, whither Geo. (Liz's brother) & Jim (uncle) had gone before us. We returned at 9-30 and said goodnight at 9-45. It was very dark, though quite fine & fair tonight. Liz's Grandmater spoke to us sometime before we went over to see the light.

The search light was for nearly two minutes directed full upon the spot where we stood, dazzling our eyes completely & making us the centre of attraction, the observed of all observers, of which there were many.

September 4th. (Mon.) [1893]

Saw Liz coming down, talked to her a bit and then … Why repeat? Liz has strict orders from her young brother Geo. to be in by 9-30 tonight. She got in I think to the second; and her Grandmater was so astonished that she on seeing her started back and exclaimed wonderingly "NIVVOR". [NEVER]

Ada had something to say tonight about Liz being to much out at nights. (Liz's exam is three or four weeks time.) Liz gets up at six and studies until eight in the morning, and at night is on from 4-30 until 8 or 7-45 doing her homework. Surely that is enough.

September 6th. (Wed.) [1893]

I went down then to the Chapel (It was still raining rather heavily) I saw Liz coming down under an 🌂 and enveloped in a cloud of grey* I just spoke in passing. I saw Jen.(Miss. T.) a few minutes later.

*Liz has got a great light chequed cloak or mackintosh or something of that sort tonight.

Thurs. 7th..

I met Liz and Jen coming down. Liz went straight home. Liz's pater was here today and yesterday. Her mother visited their abode the other day. The Grandmater says they are (at least Mr P. is) in the way and his return home was a riddance. Harry, Liz's brother, was there. Liz came out at 7 o'clock tonight (!) to avoid speaking to Mr P. (Liz's father behaved cruelly to her and to Geo – indeed to all the children– when they were at home. He had a good drapery business, but drinking almost ruined him. On account of the rough usage Liz and Geo.– especially the latter received– they came many years ago to stay with their Grandparents, who are very good to them, naturally.) Liz had a sister Sallie who died a few years ago. She was a good girl a year or two older then her sister, with long dark curling hair & dark eyes– differing entirely in looks form Liz (so Liz. said but there is in their portraits a striking resemblance). Mr P. is a teetotaller now and travels with drapery goods.

September 9th. (Sat.) [1893]

I did not get from work today until 1-10. Liz's Grandpater kept me talking? of an hour. I went over and got a sketch of the Japanese warship "Joshinokan". At 2-30 the great Chilian ironclad "Blanco Encalada" (named after the vessel blown up during the recent revolution in Chile and sister ship to the world renowned "Esmerelda") slid gracefully and slowly, though in awesome majesty into her native element, amidst strains of music and ringing cheers from the stands on the Newcastle side of the river.

I saw Liz before this, coming from School where Ada had been examining (testing) her and Jen (Miss S.). They have done very well, so far as they can state. I went up the lane at 10 to 8 and saw the little girl (whom?)

Liz. & I got home at 9-30.

September 10th. (Sun) Anniversary Services. [1893]

I did not go this morning, but read a book (and while doing so saw her washing the front step.) Liz and Jen S. were at the afternoon service - so was I, of course, not beside 'em. At six I went to chapel.

My seat was already occupied, partly by Misses P., T. and S. I had to sit on the back seat and I am afraid I did not behave myself as I ought, for I did some sketches, not being much interested in Mr Jas Ogden (Senr.) who went on until $\frac{1}{2}$ to 8!

September 16th. (Sat.) [1893]

Went down in 2-30 boat to finish riverside sketch from life. I left the picture at the landing & went to M. & Swans. I found that "The Prisoner" had been put into a handsome gold frame and looked splendid indeed, but they had made a mistake and put too good a frame in consequence of which (altho' no fault of mine!) it will be 8/- more making the cost 2/10/-. I gave him the £2/- as I was not prepared just then to pay the whole, and told them so. The gent was very kind and thanked me profusely. He can't exhibit it in their window but has it in a good position in the picture room. He said that it had been a good deal admired. He asked what price I intended asking. I thought about 10/-/- so he advised me to put it at 12/12/- and said he would do his best to sell it or words to that effect. They will send it to the Sketching Club next Saturday. Well the picture – at least the frame now looks really beautiful. The frame is about 5" deep with $1\frac{1}{2}$ inch gold slip.

September 23rd. Sun. [1893]

When I bid Liz Goodnight I said "Lizzie, give us a kiss!" she laughed and replied " No I keep them all for my Grandma!" and went off laughing.

September 24th. (Mon.) [1893]

Edward and I were astir by 4-30 this morning. It was quite dark, but began to turn grey soon after. We got on our coats (which proved handy for carrying Mss., sketches, lunches, notebooks etc. and as a secondary part was rather useful for the cold). (I had written to Liz a note, per Lily, asking forgiveness etc. for what I asked last night, commencing "My Dear Liz." and signing "Your ever faithful friend J.T." so lovingly.) Well we got on our great coats as the grey in the eastern sky was turning to yellow. It began to rain a little, but by the time we reached the Central Station, faired up. The train journey for the first part was somewhat monotonous. The same clatter drag and jolt, the identical miserable scenery; flat fields and bushes and trees, without variation, scarcely. Occasionally could be seen a cottage or a farm, some times a human being, or a group of frightened sheep. When we caught the first glimpse of the sea, we were not sorry. Alnmouth looked exceedingly pretty in the morning light. The town, although small is compact and nestling as it does under green cliffs and broken banks with its wet roofs shining bright in the mornings fleecy roseate lights, looked beautiful, indeed quite a picture. The wet sand and shallow water of the river Aln reflected the houses, making the scene complete in its picturesqueness. The train swept across the bridge with a swish and a roar and soon bonny Alnmouth was left far in our wake. Now and again we got the sea in view, sparkling in silver and grey and breaking on the great stretches of sandy beach in clouds of foam.

The scenery after leaving Alnmouth became a little more animated. We actually saw a few people staring about them. There were more farm houses, cottages, and even turnpike roads etc. At length we passed Holy Island, lying along the sea coast and shortly after, rattled across that most artificial & temporary structure, Berwick Bridge. At the station we had an hour and a quarter to wait, the time we spent having a look round. It was cold but fine; there was nothing to see at Berwick except the clean and almost deserted streets, and a statue on a drinking fountain to Jos Maclegan. There is rather a fine town hall, and an old bridge (brig). We were on the quay some short time. At 15 to 8 we started again and ran through the most lovely scenery, rustic & picturesque, up to that pretty town of Kelso. (We passed Velvet Hall where my grandfather, Robert Taylor, was Station master for many years, Norham and the old castle, Twizell, and the beautiful little winding river, Coldstream, Sunilaws, Sprouston, and then Kelso.) The surrounding scenery is simply magnificent, stretching out on all sides were fields of green, bright

and sombre, greens of every shade and tint, there were brown fields
and grey, fields of yellow and fields of ruddy hue, all interspersed
and dotted with innumerable trees and bushes, lined with straggling
rows of stunted hedge-growth, with here and there a moss covered
pool of stagnant water or limpid stream. Birds, sheep and cattle were
here, there and everywhere lending life to this enchanting scene.
Faraway, the horizon the brilliant greens softened into blues and
purple greys- and the whole landscape shimmered and sparkled in
the glorious sunshine. We passed Melrose and its beautiful old Abbey
standing silent; in grim grey ruins, against the green hilly
background. We arrived in Galashiels at 11-15 and had lunch there
at 12.

Next we got a train at 1 o'clock to Abbotsferry. Here we were
ferried across the river by an elderly lady in white cotton apron and
hobnailed boots. I think she counted her stokes as she managed the
boat so beautifully; in fact I couldn't have done better myself. She was
evidently quite conscious of her own importance, poor body. She was
honest though, for when we offered to pay her again coming back,
she told us that the first fare did for the return also. At the crossing
place the river was beautifully clear and we could see the stones in
the bed of the river only about 3 feet below the surface. We got
ashore; a few yards straight up and we turned to the left, and found
ourselves on the main turnpike road. It was one of the most beautiful
and enjoyable walks I ever had – one of the loveliest lanes it has ever
been my good fortune to see. We had a canopy of leaves overhead,
around, and leaves underneath our feet. The sun was very powerful
and the weather kept bright and fine throughout the rest of the day
until night.

We got to Abbotsford at last, and went through Sir Walter Scott's
residence; the mansion is a splendid affair, built of brownish red and
white stones, and having small bastions with spiral conical roofs, like
a miniature Holyrood Palace. There are four or five rooms, the study,
the library, the drawing room, the armoury, besides private
apartments. Many parts are designed after churches or abbeys,
Melrose Abbey, Rostin Castle and Holyrood Palace chiefly, mostly
such as the ceilings fireplaces etc. One of the rooms is filled with suits

of armour, coats of mail, targes (shields), claymores, broadswords, maces, double-edged swords, pikes etc. – a proper armoury in fact. In all the rooms are curiosities from all countries under the sun. There are 20,000 vols. of books in the library! There are pictures innumerable, mostly portraits, many valuable miniatures among them, busts of celebrated men, including busts of Wordsworth & Walter Scott himself in white marble. There are curious old cabinets & chests and all manner of (Chantry) furniture made from various famous things of historic interest. As an example there is a beautiful mahogany desk made from the timbers of one of the ships of the Spanish Armada. __ Among the pictures are paintings by Hogarth, Sir Peter Lely, Landseer, Bennett (Watercolour of Jedburgh Abbey), Sir Henry Kaburn, and many others of note. There is a valuable case of unique curiosities, containing snuff, boxes of gold, relics of Napoleon, Burns, Wellington, Prince Charlie, Flora MacDonald, George IV, Mary Queen of Scots, Rob Roy, etc. etc. We saw guns, pistols, swords, etc. of celebrated persons (mostly presented) of many celebrated historical characters, and other things innumerable which I cannot put in here. (See the list of curiosities; Pater is much interested in this second British Museum.) I was in my glory and could have stayed for days, to admire all these old things, queer, quaint & curious. I was sorry we hadn't the privilege of examining everything; the lady showing them was in a great hurry. We signed our names in the visitors book.

We came back by the ferry (the "Lady of the Lake" again in hobnail boots) and then came to Galashiels station, where we got the 6-13 train to Stow. We enquired of several "natives" (more to hear them open their mouths then anything else) for Mr George Smith, tailor. (They used to live in Dunston. Tom and others of our family have visited them since they came to Stow. Susan was a baby when they left. Now we find Susie, aged 8, John (Joan) and Lillie (Lally), all bright rosy and interesting children, speaking with a terrible "burr".) We were heartily and warmly welcomed by Mrs. Smith. The children were delighted. Susie was at Dunston staying with us two years ago, age 5; she is not much taller, however. We spent the night talking over old times, telling the news etc. etc. until 11-30 when we of course went to bed.

September 26th. (Tues.) [1893]

Of Course it rained and poured without cessation ALL DAY! Stow is a pretty and picturesque place, no doubt, but the dismal weather tended to lower its beauty very markedly in our eyes. (The town(?) is as big as about one quarter of Dunston lying scattered about, in a valley & surrounded on all sides by hills & green fields, covered with trees & shrubs.) There are three churches, two public houses, and a policeman. There is a fine old ruined Bridge, or brig as the natives call such structures, across the river Gala (Galla) Gala water. I got a sketch. There is a large finely shaped arch crossing the stream, and two smaller ones in the field. I think it has been a main road. I got a sketch but it was very cold indeed. The afternoon was spent romping with and amusing the children. Shoosan, Joan and Lally, who "Wadna gang ta skiel (School) Cos," they said" Mar Oncle Adie and Joannie are hearr." We had a high old time of it and so had the Children. It drizzled miserably all day. We had a walk at night with Mr S. to his mother's whither Joan and Shooshan had been sent for the night.

September 27th. (Wed.) [1893]

It was fine at 6 a.m. We bid them Good Bye __ reluctantly enough at 10 and came down for the 10-20 train. Mr S. came down with us. I got a snapshot sort of sketch of Stow from the Station bridge. Of course it faired when we left in the train. We were whirled along to Kelso at which place we landed at 20 to 12. We could not get into the Abbey, so had to content ourselves after making a double attempt and both times emerging in an Orchard with viewing the ruins from the wet pavements of Kelso. The ruins of the walls are a great height and very grand and imposing they look. We honoured the museum with our presence and then went into a restaurant. At 3-20 we sped along to Berwick and from thence to Newcastle, the "Canny auld toon" second to none. I got home at 7-30, Ed at ? to 11 having made a call on the way. I for my part have enjoyed myself immensely & I have no doubt that Ed did too. The children and Mrs. S. too would well have liked to come "ower to the English side". They were exceedingly kind.

October 3rd. (Tues.) [1893]
Brilliantly Bright. Beautifully fine. "Mr John Taylor, one of the youngest members of the society (Newcastle Sketching Club Picture Exhibition) has a picture hung entitled 'A Prisoner of War' Its only fault is that it is rather dark, but it gives considerable promise; and we doubt not Mr Taylor's work will be seen in the galleries before long." (Quotation from N/c Daily Journal.) This is very encouraging. I came down with the pair (Jen and Liz). It was 20 past 10 when I got into the house and the family in general asked, very thoughtfully, anxiously & kindly after my welfare. (Why I was so late etc.)

October 13th. (Fri.) [1893]
Not so cold today; inclined to be sultry. Rained a bit at night. Lizzie P. came over to our house as I was getting ready for class at G'head. She and Ada were arranging matters for her exam tomorrow. (I was particularly anxious to oblige.) Liz went at 6-15. Ada asked me tonight if I would go to the train with them in the morning; of course I was pleased and assented readily. Sent Liz a note wishing her success.

October 14th. (Sat.) [1893]
Got up at 6. Ada and I were ready when Miss. P. and Miss. S. knocked on the door. We left at 10 past 7 and walked slowly up Gateshead. Ada walked in front holding up her gamp and her dress, and leading the way, whilst we three, Liz, Jen & I, with another gamp at the opposite extremity followed in the rear 3 abreast. I made myself generally useful in explaining the great sights of the city, in carrying other sundry unnecessary articles, etc. There was plenty of time for the 8-30 train. I shook hands with all three, told the smiling and evidently quite self-confident Liz to do herself justice, wished Jen success etc. and then left. Liz had got the note I sent yesterday by AH's brother, I think because she was very nice. Well they went down and went through the awful ordeal of the Exam, the inspector being Mr Wilson. Liz says the grammar was the hardest part. She got on beautifully with everything else. Jenny thinks she has done fairly well.

I went to the life class at the School of Art this afternoon, for two hours, having first had to go to Newcastle for canvas & paper. Paid 2/6 for fee. I scarcely knew what to do, from $^1/_2$ past 5 until about 8 when I found a subject for a new picture: an incident of one of

Napoleon's campaigns (more of this after.) I went up to AH's and found he was not coming out. I had expected Liz and the others back by 8 o'clock but they did not land until after 9. I had come home and had supper and then went up to meet them. I saw them at the Dun Cow and was jolly vexed when they said they had waited of me. Ada and Jen left us and we two– well as usual. Liz was talking about her exam etc. We said goodnight at 10 o'clock.

October 17th. (Tues) [1893]

I got up at 25 past 7! It wasn't my fault I was so late, I never wakened. At 20 past 8 I went a message for Ada, to Miss. P.'s. When I arrived she had gone to School, whither I followed. She was alone in the classroom. delivered my message, and then we began to talk, while I made myself useful in cutting a hole square for Liz. Jen arrived and shortly after I came home. I left for the class at 10 past 6. I never saw either Jen or Lizzie. I had "Principles and Perspective". I saw the pair at the shop opposite the end of Redheugh Road and came down with them. After Jen had gone it was 10 o'clock and we breathed more freely. I promised Liz to be at the Band of Hope tomorrow night at 7. We got home at 10 past 10.

October 18th. (Wed.) [1893]

Got up at 6-30 this morning and finished a watercolour sketch of the 'Four Lane Ends' for Mrs. Smith of Stow (Scotland). She said she would so like a sketch of Dunston neighbourhood.

(We are rather busy in our office work just now. Stan has given up his timekeeping to young Ismay. There are many changes in the routine of the work. Mr Armstrong the new partner being the main cause.)

October 21st (Sat) [1893]

I gave Liz some papers to read. (Her Grandmater afterwards threatened to burn them, when Liz read them on Sunday, but she let fall a hint of the proprietor of the said papers, and thus preserved them from distruction) She was and always is excessively free at the "corner" & tonight was not an exception. My hand was cold tonight, but hers was very warm __ How do I know? Guess! _____

October 23 rd (Mon) [1893]

I was photographed at 7-30 this morning in the attitude of the boy messenger, in the picture I am going to paint. I suppose I would look soft, with my trousers pinned on one side, with my coat doubled under like a 16th. century affair, and with my collar up, with my mouth opening and my eyes dilated and wildly staring into space! Of course I would look soft, but it answers my purpose. I am going to pose as Napoleon himself before long! And with my greatcoat on too!! To imitate HIS grey greatcoat!!!

October 26th. (Thurs.) [1893]

I found Liz at 10 to 8, sitting alone and looking very happy on the seat, with the bright full moon shining full upon her. I sat down alongside of her. Surely, thought I, I'll get a bit cuddle tonight. But this is what happened. After talking for about half an hour on the seat, we get up and go up past Orley's and then turn down again. We meet about four people, two pairs. The moon is very bright; the wind is cutting & Liz altho' well wrapped up, looks cold; indeed she has said repeatedly that she IS cold. Presently there is silence. I say "Don't you feel cold?" and slip my left arm around her waist. She laughs, pulls off my hand and says "Be done John". I repeat the performance, urging upon her, but all in vain, the necessity of her being kept warm. I say "The wind is so cold; it will cut you in two; and you look so cold too". But she stoutly repels my advances. She is quite good-humoured; laughing and pleased as can be; yet she says "Don't John or I won't be friends with you" and gently but firmly my hand is put aside. I then say as a last resort "Give me this arm then" taking her right arm. She was however far from being offended, immensely pleased. I really did not think that she would object this time. I like her independence though. After we came down & had talked a bit it was nearly 10, so we shook hands. It was bitterly cold. She was exceedingly jolly tonight.

October 27th. (Fri.) [1893]

I went up to the class and "went for Antinous". I got a pleasant surprise tonight. The "Discobolus" which I did last year has got 1 st prize value £1. Mr Wild's 2 nd is 10/-. I am getting on very well with old "Antinous".

Mr W. says I am going to get for prizes, books on Nov 28th. Marshall's Anatomy, & Wards principles of Ornament. 21/- & 5/-

respectively. I was encored at home when I told them of the brilliant achievements of their son, & went to bed at 11 with a frightful headache. (Windy weather.)

October 29th (Sat) 1893

Miss Lydia Sharpe has been captivated in bonds of love by Joe Dinning & the feeling is apparently reciprocated. Miss Nellie Brown has netted Jack Thompson (Africa), and Jack Dixon sees in Miss Kate Scott all that is necessary. Ben Thompson and Miss Bella Noble are inseparable, as are Miss. Ada Taylor and Mr W. Maddock. I find Tom Golightly together with Miss Harrison of Swalwell, Miss Jenny Lucas with Mr W. Garven and, strange to say, Miss Bella Ellis and Mr Tom Whitfield have fallen out for 101st. time, but are done for good or evil this time. Miss Tatten has not yet found a partner, Mrs. T. doesn't know how to account for it. (Silly woman as though Jenny were not only 16). And there's John Taylor and Lizzie P! Miss Jenny Golightly has found a Bensham chap to interest her. Sam Ellis now goes with Annie Hotchkiss, who a few weeks ago was head over ears in love with Geo. Whitfild, and as Aggie H, her sister has fallen from A. Brown to give place to Hannah Hopper. I suppose we may never make sure of two remaining together for over a few weeks. Yet one thing is certain; I shall never find one whom I shall love so well as my own dear little friend Liz. P.

November 1st. (Wed.) [1893]

Liz at Sk Club Concert. We got to the rooms at $1/2$ past 7, and thoroughly enjoyed ourselves, I am sure, until 9-30. Liz was much pleased with my picture, and I was in misery the better part of the night with congratulations and shaking hands, and explanations etc. etc. There was a splendid concert and Mr Hedley would fain have had us stay longer, but we did not and left at $1/4$ to 10. We had a good old stroll down to Dunston. Liz & I had the usual handshake at 8 to 11 o'clock!

November 11th. (Saturday) [1893]

I see Pater's portrait is in the Weekly Chronicle this week. Went to class this afternoon. I got a bit work done at "Napoleon" and at 8 went up the lane. I saw Liz after I had gone up & down once or twice, at 8-10. We went up past Orley's (and past the shoe tops in mud!) and came back by 9 to the Dun Cow. We got a good bit higher up tonight then the corner, where we stood for $^3/_4$ of an hour. Neither of the Jens or AH were out tonight that we saw. (I passed little Jen myself.) Liz was so nice tonight.

November 22nd. (Wed.) [1893]

Snowed a bit today and tonight it was a hard frost. It was moonlight and beautifully brilliant. There was a frightfully cold wind, however, yet Liz & I went for a walk. (I did not go to N/cle Sk. Club.) I never hint for squeezes or cuddles or kisses now! I cannot help saying another word in admiration of dear Liz. She has so many good qualities that any of her sex might envy her. She would not let me put my cape around her. It was a gale at our backs as we came down. At a sheltering spot some little way up Athol St., Liz & I had our usual palaver; and shook hands at 20 to 10. There is to be an AT HOME on Sat first at 6 p.m. Liz is going and I? Oh of course I am going. It will be jolly, I know.

Certainly AH will be there, in fact we'll all be there! I wrote Liz's ticket tonight. Hard Frost.

November 26th. (Sun) [1893]

Went to chapel where Mr Hutson preached a beautiful sermon and Mr Ogden christened a child "Horace" instead of "Alice". Liz and I came to the Chapel railings and said our say until 10 to 10. (She is more interesting more loveable and more loving every day!)

November 27th. (Mon.) [1893]

I am Eighteen years old, 5'-5" high (stocking feet); I am getting old now, old indeed. It seems as though 18 were three years more than 17. Well the presents haven't as yet 5 o'clock begun to pour in, it is turning dark. I am eighteen and I have a splitting headache and thoughtful and benevolently disposed friends are saying "Happy returns of the day." Mater bought me a great pair of gloves and other odds and ends for which I must be grateful. I went up, with two sketches for month meeting, and saw Liz at the Dun Cow, struggling with her back to the hurricane blast. Jen arrived at 6-30 and we trudged up together. It was fearfully windy and the girls' hats were in a perpetual tremor all the time (What nuisances hats (girls) are to be sure!) We got to the Schools where I left them tacking across in the teeth of the gale.

November 28th. (Tue) [1893]

Ada and Maggie, with Geo (Mr H.) and I went up. There was a good attendance in the Town Hall. The Earl of Carlisle presented the prizes, Mr Dunn the Major took some sort of a chair, and several Aldermen spoke. As the students made their way through the crowded hall, and stepped gingerly up the precarious step-ladder unto the platform each blushed in turn, (of course I was an exception that night) and the crimson which may have mantled my cheeks was possibly, nay – probably caused by the reflection from the Major's robes. I was oblivious of everything around me. I heard the din of clapping – I did not hear any hissing. I remember the kind old gentleman in the plain clothes with the short cut white beard, Roman nose and heavily lined eyes as he bent forward, presented the books, and mumbled out some words of praise. I was thankful when I had passed the beaming Mr White and scrambled down the next step-ladder, then I began to see people moving about. (The Exhibition was good. There were several of mine hung. "Discobolus", "3 Hands", "A Head" and "A plaster group of Vine Foliage".) Maggie and Ada came away at 9 and Mr H. and I at 9-15.

I saw Liz and Jen (who had been at their class) at the Dun Cow, 9-30 and came down with them. Liz and I took up our quarters a little way up Athol St., with our backs to the wind and talked matters over as usual. It was 20 past 10 when she left me. "Why" she said, "When I go in I have to go straight to bed," so it's all the same.

December 1st. (Fri.) [1893]

Oh the snow! Fairly and truly Xmas weather. Fearfully cold and keenly frosty.

Ada has passed First Class in her last Exam; congratulations to her and confusion to her enemies.

December 4th. (Mon.) [1893]

Mr .D. is at Glasgow today, so we took advantage of the fire. It is not so cold now however. It is dull and wet weather or rather damp. Liz and Jen and I went up together to our classes and came down together. Liz is so very fond of my coat - my big coat, I mean; she buttons it for me whenever she gets a chance, puts the cape straight etc., poor dear. Her hand is softer now, I found at 10 o'clock.

December 6th. (Wed.) [1893]

I wrote a letter to Mrs. Smith at Stow, and by next post sent the sketch of the "4 Lane Ends".

December 9th. (Sat.) [1893]

I received a note from Liz this morning, per her Grandmater. It was from her Grandpater, or at least from her, but referring to her Grandpater who was ill again and did not know when he'd get back to work. I called at dinner time with his wages and he kept me talking (I was ushered inside) till 20 to 2. Liz was coming in and out the room all the time. Meanwhile I had examined the notebook which she had returned to me while there. She had made one or two alterations and had written in the back pages "Criticism of your Story" and "Criticism of Yourself". In the first she says "But I still think you flatter that little friend of yours" she says she is proof against flattery by this time. Of course I am glad my little friend is so modest, but I don't see any flattery.

"My Dear friend," so begins the "Criticism of Yourself", and then she goes on to say that Sister Ada gave me some capital advice. She further adds "There will be a great many changes in the next half dozen years. You will then find you don't want your air castles of today. Of course when as Ada predicts, you see your dark eyed Susan, and she fulfils my parts (and even more) in your life, I shall be sorry to lose your friendship. Shall also be sorry when Andrew (AH) finds he has no further need of my company. But if 'Black eyed Susy' & AH's to come yet deserve both of you, I will be content. Till then I suppose I may remain your dearest friend, Lizzie."

It is just like the dear girl. Is not that last bit really heroic?

In the letter, replying to this I began with: "My dear little Sweetheart. You say there will be a great many changes in the next half dozen years; but I shall always remain the same funny sole, dear girl, in many ways. No 'Dark eyed Susans for me unless my present one dyes her eyes, no black eyed girl for me unless the 'present tense' one finds some worthier object of her affection. If you should be sorry to lose my friendship, I should indeed regret yours forever. And so dear Lizzie, believe me to be yours ever etc."

December 14th. (Thurs.) [1893]

Exam today. Liz (Miss P.) has passed with honours, good little girl, and I congratulated her tonight later in the moonlight. (Jen (Miss S.) has got the same marks almost exactly as Liz.) Ada passed first class at her last exam; the result was known about a week ago.

December 15th. (Fri.) [1893]

The school has holiday. Liz said she intended going to her mother's today, but owing to her Grandmater being ill, stayed at home and (good little useful girl!) did the baking. She went to the Endeavour class and, at 9, came up to meet me. She tells me that her mother and father want George to go home again for good. She thinks he will go. We came to the usual place and shook hands at 10 past 10.

December 21st. (Thurs) [1893]

After tea I went up, got shorn of superfluous upper covering and then came to the concert at the Chapel, where Mr Jack Noble was presented with a purse of gold (10/10/-). AH was absent. Poor Jack was very modest and was well encored. The meeting was lively and interesting in the extreme. It was beautiful moonlight when we (Liz and I) came out at 9-20 but there was a fearfully cold with wind blowing which compelled us to beat a retreat. Then I gave her a pair of Kid Gloves with astrakhan tops, which I had bought up Gateshead, and when matters were explained, she was profuse in her expressions of Gratitude, and I felt exceedingly happy. I shook hands with Liz at 10 past 10, and said Goodnight and goodbye. She was evidently, far from being depressed. And so I have left her until __ next __ Wednesday night! Oh dear! Between the hours of 12 at 2-30 a.m. Friday morning (when I retired for the night– or for the morning) I did part of a Xmas card for Liz. After which I began to sing:

"When evenings twilight gathers round,
And every flower is hushed to rest,
When autumn leaves breathe not a sound
And every bird flies to its nest,
When dewdrops kiss the blushing rose
When stars are glittering from above.
Then I think of thee my Love,
I think of Thee My Love."

Not exactly appropriate, I agree, but it did for me; the sentiment was there. (The autumn leaf business rather spoils it for this time of year.)

December 22nd.(Fri.) [1893] 8-45 a.m.

Liz's Grandmater brought me a note; such a letter: "My dear John – Allow me to thank you again for the gloves; they are a beautiful fit, in fact they fit just like a glove, and I am greatly pleased with them etc." She says she is rather sorry to go away if, by so doing, she will spoil my holidays. "If you want company on Sunday night, don't let any of my silly sayings part you from the Jennies. You know I would never be jealous John (Good Girl!) I trust you too much for that. (Canny lass!) She asks if I will live 6 days (I think so)." It is signed "Your dear little Liz"

December 24th. (Sun.) [1893]

Christmas Eve! At chapel I was minus AH, and sat in front of the two Jennies. Mr Hutson preached his farewell sermon tonight, and a most impressive, beautiful, and eloquent discourse it was. We had a brilliant assemblage to supper and after it was all over we adjourned to the sitting room. At 10-30 the guests "cut their sticks" and at eleven I made up my mind to go carol singing. So I did. At 11-30, about 21 of us started out, 15 or 18 singers, (including myself.)

It was 12-30 and therefore …

December 25th. (Mon.) [1893]

Christmas Day had dawned when we got to Mr Coning's and sang our first hymns under shelter of coat capes and umbrella ribs. The moon, hidden all night, had come out clearly enough when we set out, but now it was hidden by thick grey clouds, whirled across the sky by a furious wind, which greatly inconvenienced us. It rained heavily too, all the time more or less. There had been singers at C's before us. We next went out to Bensham, by leaving which we found it to be about 2 o'clock. Then we went all over the village, (having had refreshments at our house). It might have been 4-30 when we got to the vestry

where a modest breakfast was prepared. I was very tired by this time but not at all sleepy. It had been sultry the first part of the night but later or sooner on it turned cold and kept our eyes open. It was 6 a.m. when I retired to rest. I rose at 10-15 and found another letter from "Your Lizzie".

It opened out: "Dear Boy," she says. "What a lovely card! ???

What a clever boy you are John! etc. etc. I am so pleased you conquered ambition one night. Don't forget I am only 16 and, you know dear, I would not like to be frivolous like some girls." (In the letter I sent, I had said "I was going to ask for something in return for those gloves but dare not.") Further on, Liz says: "As for Jen having a chance, I wrote and told her she must not try. I could not do without you. (!) I think I'll come on Tuesday and take you for a walk to benefit your health (I must be in love)." (This last bit is in her letter, remember.) She continues: "I have been waiting for your letter all day." There was a family gathering of 22 persons, young and old, at tea, and after the repast had been demolished they began to enjoy themselves.

December 26th. (Tues.) [1893]

I went up to AH's at 11-15 and saw Liz herself – Liz – coming along. I took the box of colours for AH and came down with dear Liz. Was I not glad to see her, that's all! She didn't seem to have much color yet even. We were delightfully happy – that's all I've got to say.

December 27th. (Wed,) [1893]

I got up at the usual time this morning with a somewhat heavy heart. Rowat is absent all day. Watson (Quayside clerk) was up today. I got away at 4-30 p.m. Sent little Joe with a note to Liz, asking her to come for a walk sooner. I saw her at 6 and we went for a long stroll.

December 28th. (Thurs.) [1893]

I got a note from Liz tonight at 6.30 saying she was too ill to come out and had been, and was still, in bed. Poor dear girl, I pity her from the bottom of my heart. I went to AH's at 8-30 but could not draw him. I went for a short walk and got home at 9-15 when I wrote a long letter to Liz.

December 29th. (Fri.) [1893]

Have got a bad cold, but am not laid up. I saw Liz (the invalid) sitting at the fire as I passed the window. She turned and grinned when I saw her. Ada was over to see Liz today, so was Lil and also Jen S.

December 31 st (Sun.) [1893]

It after 11 p.m. and I have just been out listening to hear St. Nicholas town clock strike the hour. The bells are ringing gaily over the water - and we might safely say that the old year is dying to slow music! 1893 is fast dying out. Liz bid us "Good Night" at 20 to 10, and I set little Jenny up home. And now it is 20 to 12. Only twenty minutes more and 1894 will begin. Pater is getting the gun ready and I will say to the Old Year: "Good Bye for ever!"

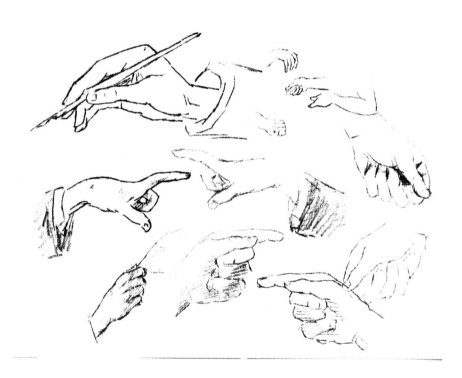

JOHN

TAYLOR,

hys

DYARIE,

(Being an Account of Incidents, — including Confessions, Flatteries, Hairbreadth escapes, Faults & Follies, Regrets, Hopes & Fears, Criticisms, etc. etc. etc., &, last, but not by any means least, LOVE-EPISODES, — occuring in the everyday life of the above remarkable Individual.)

JANUARY 1: 1894.

THE DIARY
Volume 2 - 1894 Jan - May

The Writer's Apology for <u>Writing this Diary.</u>

In case any inquisitive person happens to come across this book, and his (or her) nerves are not of the very soundest, I the writer would strongly advise the said person not to read any further. Let this warning be unheeded, and I will not be answerable for the inevitable consequences. For this is not an everyday diary – some would say it was the ravings of a lunatic, whose <u>compass mentas</u> faculties had become deranged under the influence of some person or persons not altogether unknown. The writings may be idiotic, the expressions might be foolish– I do not dispute with any such verdict, but when there is a girl on the job, I claim some allowance.

A Girl – and I mean a good girl makes a vivid and lasting impression on the mind of anyone of the masculine sex. As a rule, she can do with him as she pleases, and she has him, virtually, at her beck and call. My case is in someway Similar to this. It will be noticed that there is one particular person who figures very promineatly in these pages under the most artistic name of "Liz". I am happy to be able to say that she is rather fond of me and I of her; she is (her or anybody else's protestations to the contrary notwithstanding,) one to be proud of. Of course I am young at the art of lovemaking, and should not know how to live or what to live for if she were to go from me. I will say no more on this point lest I make a fool of myself, but a little introduction is necessary, for she is the <u>topic</u> of this <u>interminable scribble</u>.

So, I hereby make the declaration that I am of perfectly sound mind, and in possession of all my faculties, also that I have full knowledge of what I am writing. If this apology does not suffice, I ask to be forgiven; if forgiveness is unobtainable, then all I have to say is – let the hard-hearted wretch of a reader go and bury himself for reading of that which belonged to him not.

January 1st. (Mon.) [1894]

The old year died quietly as is the custom - with exception of sundry vile reports of firearms. Brother Bob, who fired our gun was our "first foot". He came in like a hero, with his deadly weapon smoking like himself (bad habit, smoking!), and wished us "A happy new Year", as did every one of the many other persons who visited us during the small hours of the morning. I went up with Mr Geo Hall and was ushered into his house and said to be their "first foot" in consequence of which I felt mightily delighted and honoured. I came home at 1 and went upstairs to bed very tired at 2. After dinner, at 1-30, I went out, having arranged to meet Miss Pugmyre, (known in here as "Liz") at that time. But it was cold and damp, sleet was in the wind – and Liz is not in the best of health just now and she did not come until 2. We had a long walk, but it was cold, although the weather remained fine.

January 6th. (Sat) [1894]

This has been a very short week to me. It was very cold all day. _ 5/- on A/c. Stanley Poad commenced work at Quayside Office on Thursday morning at 12. He is going to stay there, he says, so that is the change. Mr A. said that I would most likely have to go. Stan is going to get an advance next month. (Mr Armstrong told him so.) I expect we up here will get ditto. I commenced work at D. E. Works on Mon. April 29th. 1889 and have therefore been on 5 years come April 1894. When I came, Pater did not want me to be bound. Mr D. wanted me to be bound for four years, but as I did not expect to remain, Pater said no. I cannot say that I like clerking, nor can I say that I kill myself with working at it. Anything in the artistic line would have suited me better. Pater expects now that I ought to be out of my time, but, as I was not bound, I suppose Mr D. thinks to have his own way in that matter. However, we shall see.

January 8th. (Mon.) [1894]

We came to our dungeon (i.e., apology for an office) at 9-30. It is something horrible. We have a shed well ventilated without a fire to write in. We can't do it. We are always numbed with the cold. Mr D. won't give us a fire and finds fault when we go into the store to get warmed. I saw Liz during the dinner hour, when I gave her a note and some papers.

January 10th. (Wed.) [1894]

Travelling something of a toil. I saw Liz during dinner hour. I had got a note from her: "My own dear John" (isn't it nice!) and sent her another, with a book to read. She must be lonely just now, so I'll keep her supplied with books and papers until further orders. Liz is anxious that I should not leave off my work for her, "but" she said "you know where you are welcome." I painted at the sky of Napoleon", and at 7-30 went across to No 14, where, in her cosy little room, Liz & I had a most enjoyable evening. In spite of my entreaties, Liz got hold of this book and read it all through. How she did laugh, several times while she was reading. I told her seriously, that she must not think I had given it her for a purpose or to take any hints. Really, she knows all my secrets now. I have confessed everything. She did not say much about what was written herein but laughed heartily. She takes "Liz" as someone else. I left at 10 o'clock.

January 13th. (Sat.) [1894]

I had a good spell at "Napoleon" this afternoon and finished it for Bewick Club, 20th. inst. next Saturday (last receiving day). I received a long letter from Liz P. at 4 o'clock. It commenced "My Dearest John" again and Liz was near me for the rest of the day even before I saw her. It was such a nice note.

January 14th. (Sun.) [1894]

Liz is getting back some of her color, I think. She says she is well again. She & AH were at S.S. today – (I don't mean they were together, of course.) Jen 1 is very ill, I am sorry to say.

January 15th. (Mon.) [1894]

Here is a description of my picture,– the latest production, which I have decided to call "Napoleon at Ratisbon (an incident) "

A boy messenger has arrived from the scene of action, post haste, breathless with excitement, and mortally wounded, tells of the victory to the Emperor (who has been anxiously awaiting the results of the fight which has taken place at the town not far away). As the last words are uttered, the boy falls dead at Napoleon's feet.

The incident is very vividly described in Brownings poem, and the picture shows the boy just as he is delivering the joyful news. In the foreground stands the Emperor, as the Poem says, "with neck out thrust, you fancy how, legs wide, arms locked behind." He is in his grey coat and has a field glass in his hands. The boy standing near, with one hand clutching at his wounded breast, points with the other to the scene of action, in the distance, and excitement is, (or ought to be) depicted on his face. His horse is lower down the slope on which he and the Emperor stand. Away behind the two principal figures are grouped Napoleon's staff of Marshals and Generals, the bodyguard of their chief, and a Trooper is holding the Emperor's white horse a few yards away completing the picture.

January 18th. (Thurs.) [1894]

I am not by any means an early riser. I got up at 8-10 this morning- somewhat sooner then usual. I go to bed late – about midnight, it is 20 to 12 now! In spite of my resolves to retire earlier and get up sooner, I say to myself "Wait until the summer". I, with Rowat and Watson, had to work until $^1/_4$ to 8, at "Stock, Dec. 31/93" tonight. We had our teas sent us, per Joe A., from our house. I sent Liz a note saying I wouldn't be out until 8-30. However I hauled her out at 8 (much to her own satisfaction, I've no doubt). It used to be a long walk to Swalwell – it is nothing now for we go there every night nearly. I am sure Liz enjoys herself. Sometimes the dear girl gives me lessons.

January 20th. (Sat.) [1894]

Tom came down at 3 to put in the frame of my picture. AH and I lugged the picture across and went to quayside in 3-30 boat. We got to the Club rooms at 4.5 and gave it in. I won't know until Wednesday whether it is to be hung or not. (I think it will be all right.)

Price Catalogue is 10/10/-.

January 21 st (Sun.) [1894]

AH was not at chapel tonight and Liz was alone too. She and I went for a walk. It was bright moonlight, and promised to be very fine, (We found out differently afterwards, however.) We went up Carr's bank (first time for many months) and into Whickham, where we met the whole church congregation, which to a member – boys and girls inclusive– stared at us in the rudest possible manner, as though we were some newly imported animals for the Zoo. We came round by the fields and down the lane. Then it began to rain, for the sky had suddenly and rapidly become overcast with clouds. It rained somewhat heavier as we came down, so Liz put up her gamp, (i.e. umbrella.) I took it and while she nestled under and put her arm under mine, I held the "protector" over our shoulders, as the rain and wind began to beat furiously at our backs. This was very nice and we didn't care a rap for the wind and rain. (Courtship under an Umbrella!)

Of course we talked about nice things and nice possibilities and nice occurrences all the time. Arrived home before 9-30.

AH was with his uncle Mr Wm. Laws at Bethesda tonight giving out hymns!

January 22nd. (Mon.) [1894]

Ada is absent from school today, through illness (W.M. is poorly too, by the way), and Lily is rather unwell. Liz (Miss P.) commenced at school this morning (first attendance this year) after 1 month's holiday. She is almost herself again and sometimes has colour, besides when she blushes. Liz said she was tired of staying at home and was glad when she got back again. All the teachers in Ada's school (with the exception of Jen 2, Miss S.) have had a spell of illness within the last few weeks. (Miss L. said, when Liz was out with me one night for a walk, that she did not think Liz unwell enough to come to school, if she could be out at nights – and the next week she (Miss. L.) was off herself ill.) Liz has got some more medicine of similar hue (amber) but she declares herself to be well again. Her head has ceased its beating. We got down at 1/4 to 10. __ Oh Dear! __ Liz would talk all the night– and so would I to her, but I am afraid she might get cold, standing, and have to take hold of her hand to remind her.

January 23rd. (Tues.) [1894]

Frosty weather and very cold. I got my papers etc. from Liz's tonight. Jen 2 was there to tea. We three went up to class as usual. I met Liz again at the old place and we came home together. Of course we had the usual conversation, which is most interesting by this time of day.

January 25th. (Thurs.) [1894] 2-30 am. Owing to Ada and Maggie and Minnie not arriving until that particular time, from Mr Hutson's party (at Mr Wilson's).

I was arranging old papers again until 7-30, when I went out for a walk with my dear little friend Liz. She was just as nice as she always is, and what more can I say? The family are all very well and the relations – viz. – Mr and Mrs. Hall and little Hilda, that little imp of mischief who never had a match, as regards mischief. Then there are Mr and Mrs. Thos. Taylor, and little Tom and Ada and Alfred – known by the very poetic name of Baby Leathard. Little Ada still has her tiny nose, round chubby face and long, painfully straight hair; Tom is a bright, intelligent little chap, destined to become an artist I think for he is a capital drawer and his capability for art ought to be fostered. He often stays all night with us and I cram him with stories of Bonaparte's wars and Wellington's victories and such like, to which he is never tired of listening. Mr and Mrs. Robert Taylor are in capital health and so are their sturdy little boys, Tom and Bob, with their white hair and ruddy cheeks, dimpled faces and blue eyes. Their little brother Albert has been having a bad time of it, poor man. He has had several severe illnesses, but is now recovering from them and promises soon to be well and strong as his Saxon-like brothers.

I am wandering! I wandered up the lane tonight, bye the bye, with Liz, as I was saying when other thoughts interrupted me. We went up a good way and sat on the railings watching the scenery. There was no moon but plenty of stars. Orion was very brilliant, so was the Polar star and the big and little bears vied with their brothers in their brilliancy. Looking over towards Newcastle, it puts one in mind of a sheet of paper or board, in front of a bright light, having scores of holes pricked in it. These are the lights of the city. There is a light on the other side, on the hill top, proceeding from the window of Copeland's house and that is the only light in that direction. I was telling Liz reminiscences tonight, about when I was a little boy in the infants school under Miss McDougall and Miss Hunter; and when I used to go to the town with mother on the Saturday afternoons, through the big streets and the great markets, eating "hokey pokey" or Arkle's sugar candy. And she laughed when I told her other things

I used to do when I was "a little toddler" as she puts it. I was happy then, but am happy if not happier now. We came down and stood a bit at the old corner & then decamped. We saw her "Ganny." (Mrs. G. by the way is very "kind" with me.) I shook hands with Liz before 10.

January 30th. (Tues.) [1894]

Very cold and frosty weather today. I went up to class with Liz and Jen, as usual. Why I am forgetting the event of the day – or the night. Miss Swift (Liz's teacher who attends the school of Art) knows who I am now. I had done a sketch in Liz's book and she (Miss. S) must needs know who had done it When she asked the name of the "She" who had done it, Lis was bound to confess that it was a "he", but Miss. S. pressing her further got to know my name. She asked if I had ever mentioned her name and Liz said "Yes I believe he has, hasn't he Jen?" By this time both Jen and Liz were in hysterics, and so the thing ended. Miss. S. will begin to connect things now. She will have to be careful too!

February 1 st (Thurs.) [1894]

The wind is up again, blowing great guns. I got a note from Lizzie at 5. She was not coming out, "The lonnan was too cold" and "Their room was so <u>inviting</u>," (putting special stress on the latter word.) I went across, of course at 7-30, and Liz ushered me into her room. (It is <u>so</u> "inviting".) After it became too hot to sit in front of the fire, I coolly sat beside Liz in the chair which is always beside the one (the armchair) in which she sits. After she has combed my hair a thousand times, examined my hands, eyes, feet etc., I suddenly find that I am dreadfully sleepy. Gradually my head droops and at length finds a resting place on Liz's shoulder. What bliss!

My cheek is against hers sometimes and then I feel very very

comfortable and happy. Yes I could have snatched a kiss, but perhaps that would be carrying the liberty too far. I content myself with an occasional caress of her laughing face with its lines and dimples. I know that she is happy too, so I am glad. I wonder if she would like a kiss? A genuine "lip tickler" (without mistletoe or game). As I have said: I might have got one without any trouble, but I might have offended dear Liz and I wouldn't be rude to her for the world. Liz still wears her red (dark crimson) dress with the famous Swiss belt attached.

I am very fond of the Swiss belt. AH used to declare that it was for an arm and hand to fit round it. I won't dispute that, I put my hand round tonight, but Liz, although she didn't lose her temper I can't say that she cared for it's being there, anyway she was bound to resent the liberty in as delicate a manner possible so I took the hint and the offending member was withdrawn.

When I am looking at the sketch that reminds me that Liz has got a black jacket with cape or collar or something of the crimped pattern around the neck, so.

She has got a new dress too of the pleated pattern with an ordinary belt! It is dark brown with light splashes. Well it was 10 o'clock when we suddenly awoke to the fact that it was indeed so. I therefore got on my overcoat and prepared to decamp.

February 2nd. (Fri.) [1894]

The wind has been roaring and howling all night, it is simply disgusting. I have heard nothing from the Bewick Club. The Chronicle, commenting on it today says that there are "hundreds" not accepted, as there is no room for the great number sent in. I think I'll go and get a catalogue tomorrow.

February 3 rd (Sat.) [1894]

I went to the Bewick club this afternoon in 1-30 boat. I bought a catalogue but did not go in. I looked in the alphabetical index in the back, but alas! My brows lowered for mine did not appear thereon. The picture is rejected. I asked at the door. I can get it after Monday. And so after all my labours and expectations it is not fit for exhibition? Well, I won't call anybody harsh names. I cannot say, however that I am satisfied, for I am far from it.

February 6th. (Tues.) [1894]

Worked overtime at home again. I was never so much annoyed before. Got a card from the Bewick Club dated 30th. Jan (a week overdue). "We regret that we are unable to hang your picture" etc. "And we shall thank you to send for it between 10 am and 4 p.m. today" (Today indeed! And before 4 too!)

At 12-30 I went up to AH's (I had seen him in the morning). His Pater and he had gone into Newcastle with the flat to bring out my picture, so I toddled after them. The wind was blowing great guns and the girders of the Redheugh Bridge were vibrating unpleasantly as I stepped lightly across. I saw AH beside the Cattle Market. He was bringing home the picture. I got on the flat beside him and his Pater drove us home, Bobby the horse going in splendid style.

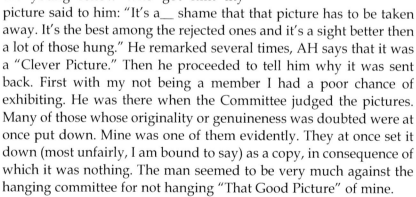

He told me what they had said. He went in and carried the picture out, having given in the ticket with which I had provided him. There were scores of rejected pictures. AH says that the young fellow who got him my picture said to him: "It's a__ shame that that picture has to be taken away. It's the best among the rejected ones and it's a sight better then a lot of those hung." He remarked several times, AH says that it was a "Clever Picture." Then he proceeded to tell him why it was sent back. First with my not being a member I had a poor chance of exhibiting. He was there when the Committee judged the pictures. Many of those whose originality or genuineness was doubted were at once put down. Mine was one of them evidently. They at once set it down (most unfairly, I am bound to say) as a copy, in consequence of which it was nothing. The man seemed to be very much against the hanging committee for not hanging "That Good Picture" of mine.

(I am very pleased and gratified to learn this; it has lifted a load somehow and I feel glad that such was the principle reason of my pictures' rejection.)

When we got it home, I at once rearranged the pictures in our front room and hung it in a good light with a decent slant.

February 8th. (Thurs.) [1894]

Oh the wind! Starlight at night and fine but Liz and I don't go for walks now; we have "At homes," in her room with a good fire roasting our left sides. At Last! I got a kiss from Liz, (or rather AT her) tonight before I came away. It was 10 o'clock, and I had my face above hers & my arms around her (no I didn't look soft!) I said "It is 10 o'clock Liz. Have I to go now? Liz replied (She does not talk like the 3d novel heroines!) "If you like." I think I hesitated a bit & then said "And can I have a kiss before I go?" She laughed and said "No" "What for? Why what do you want THAT for?" "Oh" I answered "nothing very particular, but when she asked a second time I said "Because it's nice." A few minutes elapse & we both gaze dreamily into the fire which almost black out. Then I notice that Liz has dropped her eyes "May I have one? " I ask again in a persuasive tone. Her cheek has suddenly become very hot but she has already felt herself blushing, for she says something about my making her blush. After a bit I ask again and she says gently, and with a little laugh "Well you can if you like." I wait a bit & then say "Then hold up thy head" but Liz isn't a machine. So I turn up her face with my hands and kiss her lips for the first time. That is all and it was so nice.

February 9th. (Fri.) [1894]

Pater had an interview with Mr D. today as he came from Newcastle in reference to my future "Welfare" at D. E. Works. It was most satisfactory; Mr D. won't forget me and promises to do his best for which I thank him. It was very boisterous tonight (as it had been all day) but I went out with the intention of going to class. I knocked at No. 14 to tell Liz that she had better not come to meet me as it was so stormy. She was however much surprised when I told her that I was really going to class. She then reminded me that the fire in her room was ready for lighting and that it was so stormy outside. How could I leave her; how could I disappoint the poor girl? I went inside and stayed the night beside her.

February 12th. (Mon.) [1894]

As I came to work this morning, my eyes became used quite, to scenes of ruin, wreck, devastation, and destruction. The wind has been something terrible all night (altho I didn't wake at all) and has done enormous damage all over the countryside. I went to class with Jen and Liz at 6-30. Did some clay modelling and 'Anti' Bo't tickets for the social on Friday night for Minnie and myself. Liz was at Library door as usual & we got home by 10.

February 16th. (Fri.) [1894]

Miserable, raining and blowing; we are having the elements at there worst in turns – snow and wind and rain. It is the School Concert tonight, but it is raining heavily. It rained continually all night and all day today (Saturday) it has been ditto. I went to the social with Minnie. Got to the School in a state of "dripping wet" – we lost the tram and got up before the next arrived. I had a new blue "reefer" coat on, and felt somewhat awkward for a time. There was a splendid company and the rooms (two), tastefully decorated (my work of art being– ahem! – undoubtedly an immense addition). The array was very brilliant, evening dress prevailing. Very conspicuous during the evening were the following ladies and gentlemen: Misses Swift, France, Collins, Smiles etc. and Messrs. White, Wilkinson, Phillipson, Stevenius, Forster etc. We had shadow shows & Tableau Vivants, the latter being especially good.

Mr. Forster, as showman with an elongated nasal organ, extolled the wonders of his waxwork which consisted of, (as he impressed upon our minds several times at each exhibition) the very finest in the world and had been procured at enormous expense: Little Miss Muffet (Miss F. Collins), The Queen and Knave of Nursery Rhyme renown, (Miss Swift & Mr. Phillipson, who performed their parts to perfection, "Pears Soap"), "You dirty boy" (Nicholson), "Mother Seigall's Syrup" (Nicholson & a lot of young kids). Mr. Pearson acted "The Penny in the slot & see a Prize fight" exceedingly, with Nicholson & Patrick. Mr. Tourtel was also acting a bit but not very prominently. Mr. Forster was rigged out like a country bumkin and began fishing in a little toy pail for kippers, and he was apparently delighted beyond measure when he made a "Cured" haul. Everything in the Tableau was very good.

After supper and refreshments came the dancing which continued until 11-30. Minnie had one or two dances; I had none for the simple reason that I can't dance. I am like Mr White in this respect. By the way I might say that he turned an invisible handle of one of the "box seats" for the special edification of the dancers. I introduced Minnie to Mr. Wilkinson only.

February 17th. (Sat.) [1894]

What beastly wet weather! It has rained incessantly all day. I got wet coming back from work and stayed in writing in this book. It was still raining and dismal when I went to see Liz at 7-20. Certainly she had no notion of venturing abroad "on such a relentless and stormy night." I had written a note to "My Dear Little Sweetheart" sometime before I came over.

I was introduced to Liz's cousin in a somewhat offhand manner tonight. I was actually caressing Liz and she had her arms around me when the door opened suddenly, and "my girls" namesake entered the room. Her Grandmater sometimes comes in but knocks first, but we had not expected Liz's cousin, she is so shy, she says. We got up rather hurriedly I confess– at least I did and Liz leaned back in her chair. We were all grinning (Miss P's favourite word, bye the bye). Liz half rose and said painfully: "This is my cousin, Miss Seymour," and finished the introduction with my surname, adding a prefix. Miss Lizzie Seymour didn't stay long after that. She seized a paper from the drawers tops– (what she had come to find) and withdrew, grinning still. She is tall & pale, but has a good looking, round pleasant face and a very musical laugh rather like that of my own little friend.

February 19th. (Mon.) [1894]
Bitterly keen and cold all day and moonlight after 8. Worked overtime, until 8-15 tonight. I went home for tea at 4 and then back to the office. Watson (new clerk) has, I think, been getting us (Rowat & I), or trying to, into mischief. R. was in before Mr Armstrong this morning and got somewhat wide in saying that if he didn't do enough "work down there" (as Watson had hinted, evidently), they had better get someone else in his place to do it. Mr A. was not harsh, though and he & Mr D. settled the thing amicably I believe. Mr D. doesn't like Watson at all.

I went up to Gateshead (Straight from office) to meet Liz and brought her home by 9-15. (Rowat saw her higher up Askew road!) Liz didn't want to stand outside talking, in the cold, so she persuaded me to go up to their house again. We both had woes to tell each other. Hers are school troubles, mine office hardships.

February 21st. (Wed.) [1894]
Rather cold – very thick and misty & misty struggling moonbeams at night. I went across and had the usual chat with "my lass" until 10. I dropped my old diary for 1892-3 out of coat pocket – quite unintentionally I can assure myself – accidentally & Liz got hold of it much to her delight no doubt. I afterwards heard that she found it at 11-30 when going to bed. What a find! I am rather sorry for she has read some things, which I know would hurt her feelings somewhat; I stayed until 10, as usual.

February 22nd. (Thurs) [1894]
Weather a little better then yesterday. Mr Watson (D. E. W.) complained of the fire in store being too hot, to Mr D. who informed Mr A., which gentleman in turn straightway "sacked " Thos Gardiner, storeboy in general, much to the latter' s satisfaction. R. and I stayed until 6-30. We get 1/- for each of our teas and overtime pay, we expect. I knocked at the rapper of No 14, punctual at 7-30 and Liz said "Come in". She finished her lessons and then I got back the Diary, upon the contents of which she made various comments.

February 23rd. (Fri.) [1894]
A most uneventful day. I went to class tonight in the howling storm of wind & rain, much to the astonishment of Miss. P. to whom

I had addressed a letter. I think she was much
disappointed, poor girl, but I had really to go. I almost
finished "Anti" in outline. I have been attending very
badly recently, what with bad weather and overtime and –
and–something else. Liz is anxious that she shouldn't stop
my going to class at any time. I hope to finish the color
drawing of "Anti", though to send up to Kensington.
"E. S. K." looks nice on a drawing and increases its
value. I have some of last years' drawings to bring home. I
can bring home my picture "Napoleon" now. Mr. White
has never mentioned it, rather to my surprise. I am scarcely
so proud of it after tonight. Only Mr. Fearon mentioned it
and suggested some improvements, but he maintained it was
"Splendid"– "By Jove!" he said, too, by way of emphasis, and I felt
much better. I came home by myself tonight and had a bit talk to my
friend AH, so that it was 10 (usual time) before I got home. I wound
the clock up tonight and the weight dropped through the already
damaged bottom, to the floor with a dreadful noise. It was $^1/_4$ to 1!

February 24th. (Sat.) [1894]

I had given a note to Liz saying we'd go in 1-30 boat to N/C,
Bewick Club, (she had promised to go.) but I found I couldn't get
ready in time and let her know. So we went in 2-30 boat and got to the
Bewick club rooms by 3-15. There were some really splendid pictures,
including one by Lady Butler (Miss Thompson), "E. B. 1890" called
"Evicted": an Irish picture, with an Irish woman in the foreground.
The colouring, composition, landscape, sky and grouping was
something splendid. Ralph Hedley surpassed himself in his pictures,
especially "The Breadwinner". There was also a beautifully drawn
and touchingly pathetic picture by Bacon, called "Forgiven" – a sort
of prodigal daughter returning to be pardoned by her father on his
death bed. Among the collection were pictures by Clara Montalba, M
Whittier, Hy. Moore, Jno. Terris etc.

I got Liz to go into the refreshment room, where I ordered some
tea; the gentleman left at once in a very brisk and business-like
manner. There were also two women waiters in the room beside
ourselves. We waited a few minutes and then as nothing came to

hand we began to get fidgety. We waited 10 minutes, until after 6 and still the women never once spoke to us, although I asked "Is this the refreshment room?" They replied stonily "Yes," and no more. So we waited, but feeling very foolish. So ended our first misfortune in the refreshment room; the second was even more disastrous, for after I had paid for our teas I found I had to come back in the boat– nothing! Not a penny!!!

Strange to say I didn't faint or turn pale or even swear. No; a queer sort of idiotic feeling came over me.__ I had forgotten about getting any teas and besides, did not get any change which I ought to have received at Dunston, when I got the tickets. Here I was in a fix. Then I asked "Are you going by bridge or boat?" (It was the last boat which would contain the roughs, as she had said before;) "Oh, by boat; Why?" "Oh," I said in as matter of fact sort of a way as I could assume, "because – because if I were by myself I would go round by the low bridge." Liz looked surprised. "What for?" she asked; "Have you no money?" "No" I said and I couldn't for the life of me look up, "I have nothing!"

(I don't know how I said it, but I got it out somehow.)

"Why never mind, I've got some" she answered quickly, and after a few minutes silence I explained how it was. She was kind, bless her! She made light of it, but I couldn't forget it. I got the tickets with her money (just think of it!) and vowed many vows as I came across in the boat feeling somewhat dazed. I went home "to tell them I'd come" and also to get some money.

March 1st. (Thurs.) [1894]

I went up to School of Art to get picture at 7 o'clock (trying vainly to get AH to accompany me) and found several of the students at work. Mr Pearson, whom I asked what he thought about my "Napoleon". He had a very favourable and encouraging judgement, but I wanted practice at figures. The flesh tints were rather cold too, but the landscape was good; there was much creditable work in the picture. I got it home by 8-30. Called and let Liz have a look at it. She liked it very much.

March 2nd. (Fri.) [1894]

This month of March, acting up to the old proverb has "come in like a lion" – let's hope it will go out in gentler style. Went across to No 14 at 8 o'clock and received a cordial reception. Liz looked very pale. She came home from school today at Ada's suggestion, feeling tired and unwell. She is not so very ill, but feels weak and tired, has headaches and beatings in her head and ears and that sort of thing.

March 3rd. (Sat.) [1894]

O, a lovely day. A bright blue fleecy clouded sky– but the worst of it – wind – a high wind. I saw Liz when I came home. She said, "Isn't it a beautiful day!" I echoed it. She was going for a walk too, and I wanted to ask her to go! All right; 2 o'clock, we went and had a good outing; it put us in mind of old times. (She still wears her red frock and Swiss belt after all that has been said to the effect that they were to be at last, forsaken) We got back before four.

March 5th. Mon. [1894] Ah! I got a kiss tonight, and felt supremely happy when, with my arms round her neck and waist I felt her warm lips against mine.

March 7th. (Wed.) [1894]

I nearly met with an accident today. As I was going up the yard a lad accidentally flung a white hot rivet in front of my eyes, across my path, almost touching my left eye; it felt warm for a moment in that region. I never even looked back to see who had done it!

March 9th. (Fri.) [1894]

A splendid day. I saw "my Liz" today as I went to work at 1 o'clock. She had a bell in her hand and was wringing it noisily. She grinned and rang the louder when I came into view, and when I grinned, she hid herself behind the stone gateway; and the bell ting-a-linged in my ears for a good bit after, while I laughed to myself and then at the children as they rushed head over heels to get to school in time. I wonder if Liz takes pity on the poor kids when she fancies what she must have been?

I saw her again at 6-30 when I went to class at Gateshead. She had a headache and was going to stay in.

March 12th. (Mon.) [1894]

Liz and I went up to class together. I commenced with "Anti" in colour, and had ½ hour spell at same. I gave in my name to be examined in the following subjects in April: Perspective, P of Ornament, Clay modelling (elementary) 3rd grade Freehand (drawing ornament from cast), Life, & Shading models, six subjects I hope to pass well in ALL. Liz was waiting for me when I came out, at 9-10. She amuses herself until I come with watching the girls in the rooms above dressing and coming out.

March 14th. (Wed.) [1894]

Liz and I went to the "Diorama

Exhibition" at Bethesda Chapel, Gateshead tonight. We got up at 7 and took seats in the gallery. Commenced at 7-30. "A Scamper round the States– Chicago Exhibition" and "Pompeii" were given, besides sundry views. The Choir sang a Glee and "Rock of ages", Mr. Soulsby charmed us, and Miss Wheatley sang "Killarney" in first rate style. Got out at 10 o'clock. The Misses Henderson were there and they saw Liz and I, and I guess they'd say something to each other about us. Liz and I got home by ¼ to 11.

March 15th.(Thurs.) [1894]

Worked until 7 tonight and went to Lizzie's at 7-30. I was somewhat surprised at the colour she sported in her hands and cheeks. I was very pleased to see it; it is a much better sign. And she was her old self again – so nice, so pleasant, so gentle, so kind– bless her!

March 16th. (Fri.) [1894]

I was astounded when I heard this dinner hour that Liz was not at school – ill in bed! Astonished and mortified. How she suffers, she who is so good and uncomplaining, so patient. I wish I could take it away; how willingly would I bear the pain in her stead! I have never yet had an opportunity of displaying any act of self-sacrifice for Liz's sake, but I hope to prove myself her worthy protector if ever occasion offers. I have wandered again_ but then, this is the diary of John Taylor.

I went to see Liz tonight before I set out for the class. She was in bed and but for the handkerchief round her head did not look any worse then usual.

March 18th. (Sun.) [1894] PALM SUNDAY

A year ago today I was strangely disturbed. A certain little girl for whom for many days I had cherished my best affections, had taken such a hold on my thoughts that I was continually thinking of her. How I longed to speak to her only I knew. Well I know that dear girl now. She was sitting on my knee caressing me and I kissed her too, just tonight there!

March 22nd. (Thurs.) [1894]

Found myself sitting beside my lady friend at 8. She is still the same dear little girl. Her eyes are as bright as of yore, those eyes "that sparkle bright in liquid blue", & her mouth is always dimpled with smiles. Her loving nature is unchanged– on the contrary it is more loving every day, therefore I say again, she has no equal in this village at any rate.

Lizzie's brother Willie (age 6) was in tonight. He has a round ruddy face, a tiny nose, dimpled cheeks. a laughing mouth, fair hair and bonny blue eyes – also I might add, he is most mischievous, making the door rebound with his repeated knocks for admittance denied him. Liz made many confessions tonight. Kisses at 10.10. Handshaking at 10.11.

March 26th. (Mon.) [1894] Easter Monday

I remember last Easter Monday perfectly. I painted a dog in the morning, and ran out to see Miss Henderson's marriage. In the afternoon I saw Liz and Jen. Miss P. and Miss T., several times. Liz spoke, much to my delight, when I was standing at the foot of Havis field "studying sunsets". Did not go outside this morning. I painted backgrounds in portraits instead. I ate an egg before dinner a "paste'n" and came out with Liz at 1-30 o'clock.

We went into the "Wonderful Forest", and took our seats first on

the grass up the hill and then on the railings dividing it from the fields. After we tired of the "forest" we wended our way uphill and then came down through the field where we sat on Saturday and out at the bottom onto the main road again. If little Willie had seen us then what a story he would have had to tell his "Ma". His tale was awful enough as it was. He said "Gramma, do you know when I was in bed last night, when our Lizzie thought I was asleep, I saw her put her arms around John Taylor's neck & he had his cheek close against hers!"

March 27th.(Tues) [1894]

I have a sad occurrence to put down here. I am sorry although it might turn to my advantage. Rowat did not come to office this morning, and Mr D. was in a rage. R. sent a telegram, which I did not see but I guess it would be an excuse. However, Mr D's reply was short and sharp, (if not sweet). It ran thusly "If not here today, can stay away all together." There was a second telegram from R. later. We gave over for the day at 12. Joe A. had instructions that R. must put in a half day, (same as us) if he came that afternoon. R. <u>did</u> come but was in a bad state. He left a letter which has lain until now (Wed) unopened.

Wednesday 28th

When R. landed this morning he seemed much cut up and apparently felt his position. Mr D. said to him "I don't intend you to start again, Rowat," and that was all. He repeated it twice and R. said "All right" and went into the storehouse. At 12 he went away.

March 29th. (Thurs.) [1894]

The weather continues fine but it is rather foggy. Rowat has not come to work today, I think he must be done for good: I am very sorry.

March 31st. (Sat.) [1894]

Went down by 8-30 boat to Newcastle for wages. Back in 9-30 boat. Rowat was up today and Mr D. lectured him for nearly an hour in the next office. I don't know whether he is coming back or not. Paid our salaries today. £3-12-0 as usual.

I saw Liz before I went to Newcastle in 2-30 boat and promised to be back before 7. I bought some color & brushes at Newcastle and a silk handkerchief for my girl (birthday April 4). I sent the handkerchief across with a note by Lil. Painted at the "Old Lady" until 7 when I went out for a walk with Liz. I think she likes the handkerchief. We stayed indoors until 10. When I was about to go Liz seemed to think that she owed me a duty for she said quietly and sweetly "Shall I give you something for that pretty handkerchief you bought me?" (I think I said "yes") So we stretched out our arms (and necks) and Liz kissed me. I said goodnight at 10-10.

April 1st. (Sun) [1894] All Fools Day.

I have made a __ of Minnie so far. I wrote some poetry this morning!

April 4th.(Wed.) [1894]

Lizzie Pugmire, 17 today (and dull weather notwithstanding)

To Miss L.P. on her 17th. Birthday, April 4 1894

She's neither tall nor stately, tho' she has a girlish grace

My loved & loving little friend, but look you in her face,

Is clearly seen such happiness, contentment, joy & love,

As might soon make the angels in the realms of heaven above,

To envy her; my life, my hope, my all in all on earth;

The girl to whom both smiles & tears were selfsame since her birth,

I never met a happier lass, a girl with brighter smiles,
Or one so kind & good & true & guiltless of all wiles.
No temper, jealousy or pride are ever to be seen
Upon her face– look when you like– the sweet face of my Queen
And on this bright & gladsome day of April Ninety four,
When Natures works are budding forth in rich and bounteous store,
I hail the birthday of my Love; she's seventeen today,
Heaven bless & long preserve her life to cheer us on our way
With best wishes & many happy returns J.T.

How does it read and rhyme? I do not flatter my little friend I don't. Love may be very blind but it isn't so blind that it cannot tell a good girl from a bad one. I sent a note to her tonight by Jos. Soulsby, and left another containing the above sonnet at 8, when I came home. I got across, after tea, at 8-30 – rather too late. She was cutting out I think, but soon put her work away when I sat down. I am partial to praising her good qualities, but I don't like to be <u>flattered</u>; and she occasionally embarrasses me; I think I <u>can</u> still blush a bit. Liz referred to a year tonight, when she used to dread getting too intimate with me.

I took my departure at 10-10, rather late I must confess but not so late as my "big sister", the deep tones of whose loved ones voice were wafting across on the still night breeze (poetical), as she lingered over her "Good Night"!

April 5th. (Thurs.) [1894]

We are working desperately hard at the office just now, trying to get "up to date"; therefore it came to us as a surprise, the news that we could have a <u>half day holiday</u> this afternoon. <u>Prince George is visiting Newcastle</u> (the freedom of which city he was pleased to decline!) and opened the Rutherford collage. The weather was lovely all day. It put us (Liz and I who went for a walk of course at 2 o'clock) in mind of that delightful June day last year when Prince George was married to Princess May (when I sketched Liz on the seat). We had a splendid time of it, my girl and I.

"I liked that last piece of poetry you wrote" she said tonight, and I felt pleased. I "cut my stick" at 10 o'clock. W. M. was just leaving our front door, whence he had been seeing Ada –leaving in a most uproarious fashion, singing and howling, bad boy! We two, feeling something like culprits, quietly closed the front door on us and withdrew into the darkness of the passage, until all was quiet outside. Liz hugged me before I went & I kissed her after the usual fashion. (I can't keep count of the kisses now, not at all!) What would Jen 1 say?

April 8th. (Sunday) [1894]

The choir rendered the cantata "Ruth" this afternoon for the benefit of the Gateshead Hospital. It was very nice – the second time it has been given. After this Liz and AH and I went for a walk. We didn't get home before 5-10, and were at chapel at 6. Mr Thompson preached. Liz and Jen and I went for a long walk in the thick mist which has been showing itself more or less all day, but was very bad at night. We got back at 8-30.

I am really being talked about.Apparently, various members of our numerous family have been interviewed respecting the truth of the rumoured statement that "John is going with L. P." One of these accommodating interrogators has kindly ventured an opinion on the matter; viz: "That John has looked <u>below</u> his level." Ah! I feel angry with the lady or gentleman who ever it was, but then they don't know my girl; they don't know what Liz is. I fancy it is a lady and if that be the case, who ever she is, whether she be high or low or middle on the social scale of life, she is not so good as Liz. I am glad to say however that all our folks have a decidedly high opinion of Liz, but only that she is rather young.

April 12th. (Thurs.) [1894]

So hot today that we opened the office doors and windows, but Mr D. thought it best to keep out the "draughts" so closed the windows. Commenced work at 8 am. & was on until 6 after which I went to class and had an hour's sketch at Discobolus for practice (Antique exam) . Liz came up and met me and we came home together as usual.

April 13th. (Fri.) [1894]

Cold all day. Worked extra as usual. I went to class at ? to 8, & was at Discobolus again. Mr. White says the design for the G. O. P. was "very excellent". I met Liz again. She was exceedingly happy tonight, and expressed her thoughts afterwards. We came to the corner and talked a bit and then shook hands. I miss the kiss very much! It has come to a sudden termination. At one time I used to be glad of a sight of the girl with the long plait of light hair over her shoulders, called Lizzie; next I was delighted at the prospect of Sunday coming after I had known her a few days; later I was drawn up the lanes, to find her and felt supremely happy in her company. Later still and I was in raptures because she really showed some slight affection for me. After that she used to allow me to arrange meetings, and even came herself to find me & O, what bliss! We became fond of each other and I loved as I had ever done, with love incomparable. After this I was in seventh heaven of delight when she let me take hold of her hand and then a little later, put her arm in mine. I was never so happy though as first time I put my arms round her neck and kissed her sweet face, after which she kissed me! This is the story. – I only hope it will end like the story books: "And they were married and lived happy ever after."

April 15th. (Sun.) [1894]

Fine day, everybody is saying so we must go by the majority (like the old woman, the landlady, who always said to her lodger when he came in at night, whether the weather was fine or vile – "Now here's an evening."). Did perspective this morning (!) Sunday!

April 16th. (Mon.) [1894]

Began work at 8 am. It rained in torrents in the afternoon. At 5 I sent a letter (per Jos. S.) to Liz – a long'n.) I said if it continued wet, we'd have an "at Home". (Break the rule!) But it faired beautifully at 7 o'clock. Liz and I met at Dun Cow lane and went for a walk. It was dark and ominous looking, but quite warm and no rain fell. I put my arm round her waist or neck or she places her arm in mine, but when anyone approaches we are in the habit of dropping those members, and I look angelic and innocent. We went up a long way and sat on the railings. At 9 we came down, very close together, and I kissed her when we got to the darkest place. (Paid 3/6 to Mr H. for photos.)

April 17th. (Tues.) [1894]

We are getting up to date rapidly now, at office. Mr D. is still unsatisfied apparently. After 6-30 I went to class for P of ornament and Perspective. Next class for this next Wednesday. Exam for clay modelling Tues. I came down part of the way with Kettlewell, and then with Lizzie home, I gave her instructions in model drawing and then said "Goodnight!"

April 23 rd (Mon.) [1894]

Commenced work at 8-10. I work hard there now! Went to class for Clay Modelling at 7-30., and had a good spell. I think I will get the hard one tomorrow night for exam; I think I will pass though. Kettlewell made a splendid drawing of Discobolus tonight; and Mr White said many complimentary things about the boy with a large portion of nose. (He is like M. W. Turner).

Liz was waiting and we came down together. She was careful to say that she hoped I'd pass on Tuesday night at the exam.

April 24th. (Tues.) [1894]

This day celebrated for exam in Modelling in Clay. I "arrove" at ¼ to 7, and all was ready. The noble major arrived at 10 to 7 and looked as he was very genial. Major Woolner, same examiner as we had last year has, as his name denoted, a very liberal portion of "wool" on his head. He is a fine looking old chap however, of the old school type, having a great square beard and hair shaded straight back over his forehead. We were not long in commencing operations after Mr White

y.ͤ Cast.ͤ   y.ͤ Courageous MAJ OR.

had introduced the gallant Major. Turnbull and I were together, same as last year & had the same cast. It was a rather difficult one, (different, but easier to the one we had expected,) being of a floral, conventional nature. Turnbull was in the dumps I think. He got a very fair model done however. (He had a sponge, though he never used it, and yours truly, remembering last exam, refrained exceedingly and with heroic fortitude from using the aforesaid highly dangerous though none the less necessary article. Major W. came round at ½ past 8 and made notes mentally (he must be the possessor of a good memory for there were about 18 of us!). He had a catch at me again this year, had the examiner. He asked my Christian name, &and I answered absentmindedly "John Taylor", whereat he smiled violently and laughed with exceeding great joy. He is a very jolly person without doubt; but I will set him down as a much jollier person in every way if he will give me a first this time for I'm sure my modelling deserves it. Mr Wild came to see them and thought my work was the cast. So I ought to get an excellent for that! I got mine finished, but not exactly completed; yet was quite satisfied with it. I don't think there are any failures. Major W. remarked that the standard of modelling was much better this year then last. I thought then it was a pity I was in last year. I got home at $^1/_2$ past 10 (smelling of tobacco), I got a glimpse of Liz today at 12 o'clock. She will have been lonely tonight poor girl. It looked terribly ominous today at $^1/_2$ past 3, and rained desperately for an hour or so, after which it cleared up beautifully for the rest of the day.

April 26th.(Thu.) [1894]

Same rain at the usual hour, 3 o'clock. Commenced at 8 & ended at 6. I am always dead tired now, when I get back from class at 10 o'clock. They are saying I am very white and getting thin etc.! How sad! I wish the exams and overtime were over and then heigho! for the lanes. I attended class and commenced a charcoal sketch of Germanicus, (The Orator.) Liz had a practice exam at her school tonight. She is scarcely satisfied with Miss Swift. Of course it is too late now (this is the last!) but Miss S. isn't cut out for a teacher of drawing; she has no patience or the right sort of energy. I was actually talking to Miss Collins (Louisa-Florence!) tonight – she was immediately in front of me. I met Liz and Jen, and Liz and I came home together; I carried the drawing boards! We got home by 10.

April 28th.(Sat.) [1894]

I commenced a sketch this afternoon from a description in the "Chronicle" for competition, but did not finish it to my satisfaction. I had intended to take it to class to shew Mr.White but didn't. I went to find Liz at 6-30 instead. She had put on her new blue velvet dress in readiness for tomorrow, but had brought of 3 buttons (she must be

getting stouter), so had them to sew on, after
which she would come up to meet me. I had
a parde [sic] up and down the lane, up by
myself and down with our friend Jack Tulip.

He has been going in for an exam for
"Mathematics and Steam power" etc. and
has failed, but there is great credit due to his
perseverance. I admire his indomitable
pluck, for he is not disheartened and is
going to sit again shortly. Jack T is a
bosom companion and was astounded
and grieved to learn that his friend, Bob is
finished at the Electric light works. (Robert
got his notice to quit today. As the matter of fact
however, the Co. is almost collapsed. Robert was the last fitter kept
on.) "John" said Jack in that deadly earnest voice peculiar to him.
"John, I knew there must be something a lon-ng way wrong at that
place when your brother Robert was done!" (That is a tribute – and a
deserving one without doubt, to Robert's well known skill in the
engineering line.)

May 1 st (Tues.) [1894]

A beautiful day until afternoon when, as is the custom now it,
rained. Paid £3-12-0 this afternoon. When Mr D. gave it to me he said:
"Mr Armstrong and I have been talking this matter over about an
advance for you, so he wishes it to remain over until the end of June,
when he will do something for you." (Very good.) Of course I must
behave myself etc. during this period. Pater doesn't say much.

Worked until 6 o'clock. Sent a note to Liz. It is her Drawing (Modal
and Freehand) Exam tonight – at Miss Swift's school in Whitehall
Road. She was on from 7 to 8 with Model, which she did not get
finished, but a drawing all the same. From $\frac{1}{2}$p 8 until 10
she did Freehand (with Miss S., Jen 2). The latter was
fairly easy and Liz got in the general form and
partially lined it in. She doesn't think she has
done very well, but I hold she has. We'll see
presently– in July! (What a beastly wait!)

During this time I had met with some adventures. At 8 I "arrove" at the School of Art. The exam for model and freehand was going on at our school and the ladies and chaps were tumbling out of the room as I looked round. I had brought the painting of the "Old Woman" (Mr White suggested an improvement of the eyes, so I bring it back home) and I had also brought for his inspection the sketch I did for the Chronicle Competition on Saturday. (He asked why I did not bring it last night – and an exam too mind!)

The Drawing is about 2ft x 18″ in pen & ink, containing two figures – a student, "bowed low in supplication" before the Goddess of Study. He begged that he may retain his eyesight which is becoming fatally impaired with constant and unavoidable study. Mr W. said it was splendid and said at once "Take it now to the Chronicle (?) office. Go at once! It will be better by a long chalk then most of those sent in. Put your name on and go at once!" And so I went and handed it in. I took plenty of time in walking from Newcastle up to the Whitehall Road schools, smoking and thinking. Liz came out at 10 but I lost her for a time and it was not until $^1/_4$ past that we left together, I carrying the drawing boards. It was 11-15 before Liz and I got hold of each others hands to say "Good night" when I kissed and left her.

May 3rd. (Thurs.) [1894]

I am quite an early riser now. Commenced work at 8 and go on until 6. Am getting quite rich too. I got away at 4-15 however. Got the loan of T. Buckton's board and T-square this dinner hour for the exam. I left at $^1/_2$ past 5, went up part way in tram & then after some trouble managed to find <u>Alexandra Rd. School.</u> It was 10 past 6 when I got seated all of a perspire. The room was well crowded and about a dozen examiners (more or less) were silently and grimly parading the room.

Perspective Exam.

The questions were rather stiff. We could only attempt 3 in practice and 3 in theory. I got 2 of the former worked out. One was a hectagonal frame and I got it done beautifully, I think.

The next was a cone which I got wrong and had to alter; but I think this was very satisfactory too. I was very careful, and they looked right. The theory may have been easy, but I am not good at theory. I answered 3 queries. The four hours was weary but went all too quickly. There was a continual clatter and tumble of board and squares and instruments all the time, and scared faces looking from time to time at the pointers of the clock. The room began to get cleared at ? past 9. It was 10 to 10 when I gave in my papers. I had attempted a pentagonal cone but couldn't do it. I only got a few lines of the latter in. Well – I hope I have passed.

I got home, having come down part way with a lady, not Liz, or not even a girl - O, an old married woman who wanted company, so my dear won't be jealous, will she?

May 5th. (Sat) [1894] Now this is a lovely day.

After dinner at 2 o'clock the Procession of Band of Hope & Sunday school Children left the Chapel, with pots and 2d's. (Liz had advised me to take a "pot and 2d" but I forgot both!). The Throng was headed by the Wesleyan Brass Band and the New Banner. This latter piece of work is a work of Art from the hands of our worthy friend, Mr. Ogden. It is of dark ruby satin, about five feet broad and a little more in length, the end of it being triangled thus:

On the right side is painted in Old English letters in gold "Methodist New Connection Sunday School", and in smaller text, "and Band of Hope". The whole is tastefully ornamented with flowered work. On the back is painted lilies & leaves and a Cross. The banner is fringed and tassled as usual, and is bound with blue cords to a blue cross pole supported by an upright one on either side. The poles are blue and gold. The whole thing is a veritable work of art and Mr O. ought to congratulated on its success.

The banner was planted in the field when we got there. I had joined the band etc. at the Dun Cow and had a good "graft" holding one of the cords of the banner. There was a slight fall of rain in the afternoon but it kept wonderfully fine all the time until after 8. There were smoking concerts (!) limited to three in number of persons engaged, and kissing rings. I never thought I would have gone in but I did. This was after tea. The children were fed first as usual, amidst universal washings and eating of teacakes.

Lillie went on a message to Scott's (Butcher's) this morning and on the way lost a sovereign and the purse containing same! Clever Girl!

May 6th. (Sun.) [1894]

Now it was fine all day, and the new dresses came out in consequence, Lillie and Liz among them. Liz looked decidedly nice today. The dress is "peacock blue" (Prussian blue) and fits tight. (She has such a smart waist, so she says.) She is wearing the same old sleeves (old style I mean) – viz. – balloon like at the shoulders, etc. not outrageously so of course, just nice. She is wearing the same hat as last summer. Its diameter cannot be under 16 inches; therefore 16 x 3 1/7 (pie) *sic* makes the circumference – allowing for the slightly elliptical shape – 48 inches. It is pretty though and I think Liz suits it. (It is handy for the wet,, although its light color might be spoilt thereby.) I saw all this in the afternoon. We parted very reluctantly tonight, I can tell you, but she let me kiss her "on the cheek" before saying "Goodnight".

May 7th. (Mon.) [1894]

The day has gone over as usual except for the Exam tonight. It was Shading Model this time. The examiner did not arrive until 7, so the clock was put back 10 minutes, and at 7 by it, we commenced operations. The Models which he set, as per his printed paper was as follows:

The sketch isn't very clear, but there was a cone, the small cube & the skeleton or framework cube. I was finished at 9-30, when the papers were collected and am quite certain of the best award. I don't think many were finished. The skeleton affair is hard for some of them to do. I came down part of the way with Kettlewell.

May 8th. (Tue.) [1894]

Rather fine all day. Went to class at 6.10. I had seen Liz and Jen 2 at 5-30 and had arranged to go up with them at 6, but they were to prompt for me and we went up in two bodies. I was drawing the nude model until 9. When I had crossed to the opposite side of the street – to go round by the more lively way so as to let the time slip before 10-30 when Liz's exam would be finished. I was surprised to hear the musical voice of that young lady calling me back. I stopped abruptly in my headlong career and explanations were at once enquired for and forthcoming. She had gone up with Jen to the Whitehall Rd School quite prepared and ready for the examination in Mathematics, but they found the place deserted except for Mr Miller (their tutor) who informed them, very pleasantly no doubt, that the Exam wasn't until <u>tomorrow</u> night, <u>Wed 9th</u>. Liz & Jen declare that he said the 8th. of May & I had put it down as such too. It is a great pity, when they were prepared so well for it, but Liz is going to pass of course! We came home by the Gas yard tonight. It is a less frequented way, and I could give her a bit cuddle too, you see.

May 9th. (Tue.) [1894] sic

Antique Exam. I had a "set" to get away tonight. Mr D. hasn't the power he used to have. They are most particular about our being punctual there now. What are we coming to! Got off at ? to 5! Arrived at School in a great flurry at 6 o'clock. We had to do "Germanicus" (The Orator). There were three of us. Messrs Walter Fearon, Tourtel & myself. Mr. T. was finished by 9-15 & got a good side view done. Mr. F. did not get on very well. I finished mine (all except the drapery which I only blocked in.) I think I have passed fairly well. (Got an excellent.)

As soon as I had cleared the precincts of the School of Art, I made for the School in Whitehall Rd, where Liz was being examined – and Jenny S. They didn't put in an appearance until 20 to 11; Jen left us at the Red'h B end. We couldn't very well go further with her it was so very late – but someone ought to have come to meet her. Liz and I came straight home and arrived at 20 to 12! Liz thinks she had passed well in Mathematics. They are always referring to Liz in our house now just for my especial benefit and edification!

May 9th. (Thurs.) [1894] sic

Office work monotonous. <u>Life Exam</u>. I managed to get up to the School by 6 o'clock, & had a 4 hours spell! Just Fancy! There were seven sitters. The model – nude – was in a very difficult but not uncommon pose. (Something like the "sluggard".) He was  in a somewhat strained attitude with his hands clasped behind the back of his neck.

The following gentlemen sat which means "stood". John Snee, who did not get on very well but got finished. Mr. Tourtel who made a well finished study. Then (in turn) came "me" (who of course got a drawing done but can't be certain of the results, although I did my best.) Near me on my right sat Mr White who has been ill but is now much better. He of course did a splendid one. Then Sebastian Kates and Kettlewell. The model had frequent rests, but was nearly asleep by the time 10 was up. Mr.White finished and went away at 9. (Of course he passed.) I bid goodbye to the school tonight until next summer.

May 13th. (Sun.) [1894]

Whit Sunday Very fine and promising good weather for the holidays. (I have got two days actually.) I say it was rather fine in the morn; but rained in the afternoon a bit, well after 8 I mean at night. I was at Chapel this morning to hear Mr John Maddock preach; he was exceedingly good. His appearance is very like the lads, slightly built dark and young looking.

May 15th. (Tue.) [1894] Whit Tuesday

Last night we had tried to arrange a trip somewhere today, but at 10 p.m. we found we were little nearer our settling the question then when we had commenced. However after I had written a letter to Rowat, I wrote her and told her that we'd go in the 11-30 boat (with Lily, who afterwards decided not to go) – to Tynemouth. She agreed of course; (she had said yesterday that she'd go anywhere I went or do anything I wanted, and so!), and so and so we went. By Jove, I can't forget this day. It was very dull all day, but that didn't inconvenience us at all. It was dreadfully cold going down, on the water, but we came back in the train which was very much better, quicker and warmer.

Last time Liz and Jen and I went down it was a delightful day, and we remembered it today; we had reason it was such a contrast. We landed first on the pier and went into the town. Liz had had dinner before she came away and would not come in for any more, so I satisfied my hunger and then we had a bit more tramp about. We visited the scenes of our former visits work of destruction, namely the seats on the banks facing the sea, where we found all our initials carved in the wood and Jenny's name in full. We wandered around a good bit; the station is the best part of the town – I don't mean the Police station. The Railway Station, which is spacious and beautifully decorated with shrubs and plants. We had tea in a crowded tea room and then tried to lose our way or ourselves several times but failed through the kindness of strangers. The 5-40 train was crowded, so we failed to get seated therein, but we got the 5-46 express beautifully, as Liz would say, and came home in her (the train of course.) We went through the long tunnel too. I did not think of it at the time or I might have kissed my hand loudly in the dark (!) so I there missed a point. I began to grope about though and touched Lizzie's nose end in my manoeuvres to find her cheek. She was smiling too when we got into the light. Joe Dinning and Miss Lydia got out at the far end. Ada and Wm. had come down with them – we had seen the last mentioned people in Tynemouth and spoken to them. Joe and Lydia had not wanted to come away so soon as Ada came so they separated. We had been on the sands and the grains were on our clothes still as we walked home.

THE DIARY
Volume 3 - May 1894 - Aug 1895

May 20th. (Sun.) [1894]

At 1-30 p.m. the rain and sleet and hail were coming down in perfect sheets, and at 3 the weather was beautifully fine. I got somewhat tired of S. S. this afternoon. AH has a class of his own now – so has Liz; Miss P's is in the choir seats beside the Pulpit! Stayed in with AH at the teachers' meeting until 4 o'clock, and Miss P. had to go for a walk by herself.

There is to be a Christian Endeavour Trip to Morpeth on Sat first at 2 p.m. from Central station Newcastle. AH is going, I am going, Liz and Jen 2 are going as well; a jolly lot.

May 22nd. (Tue.) [1894]

The weather is much better. A blue sky is somewhat peculiar just now. I have nothing to chronicle except the fact that I (We, that is) went for a walk after the usual fashion. Overtime Still!

May 23rd. (Wed.)

I wrote to the "Art Photo. Co.", Oxford St. W. for catalogue. At last the inspiration has come and I have hit upon a happy subject for a new picture. Well, rather ambitious again; wouldn't be me if it wasn't. But never mind, I like to tackle something extraordinary. The subject for this "canvas" is to be "Canova's Lion". So no more at present. I called to see AH tonight and did not get home until 8-15. Here I was delayed until 20 to 9 or so when I went out to find my lass. Ten o'clock boomed forth from Newcastle as we came down the lane. It was really too late.

May 26th. (Sat.) [1894]

It was quite fine at 7-30, and at 8 when I put out the notice for the preachers tomorrow, but at 8-30 the rain was coming down in torrents. I went to Quayside as usual. I got away before 12 as we had to catch the 12-30 boat. AH, whom I went to see was most emphatic in his resolve not to go now, as it had rained. (He who was so full of it last week, and he didn't go!) Miss Kate S. was going; so was my Liz, and of course I must needs say ditto. I am her willing slave – still! We got the 12-30 boat. Some of our other people went in this boat, to get a train for Blyth (where they stay till Monday night, much to T. T.'s annoyance!). Maggie had gone in 12-15 boat with the firm intention of accompanying the trip to Morpeth, along with Miss Blenkinsop, but alas! For human (female) endurance __ it was to cold for them (of course it wasn't cold at all!) so the train went off without 'em.

The seats were not of the most comfortable kind but we had plenty of room. The sky was gloriously bright all the time and the weather fine until latish in the afternoon. Miss S. was in our carriage, I mean, both the Misses S. (Kate and Jenny 2) besides Liz and I. We arrived sooner at Morpeth Station then we had expected, and in consequence, those girls got into something of a flurry. The first place of interest (!) which we visited (like a flock of sheep) was the Churchyard (ugh!), then those other people strayed away in "twoses and threeses", (in the same direction of course) and Kate went off leaving me in possession of her "gamp" and return ticket; so while Liz and Jen sat down in a great green field, I ran after the main body of the caravan and gave back Kate her belongings. I returned to find the girls seated where I had left them. Now we were alone. (Arthur Hopper, D. Watson and another chap had gone somewhere else themselves. They enjoyed their trip too; were fishing out of the river dead fish etc. and sweethearting country maids all the time!) We followed up, looking in vain for the main body; the Exodus had taken place and we were left to our own sweet will. We ought to have followed up close. We went through a wood, downward to the river, which we skirted for some yards and then crossed a red, iron-girdered bridge with a lamp hanging precariously in the centre overhead and found ourselves in the "Toon".

We didn't know our way of course, we three weary wanderers (a lad and two lasses, i.e. three idiots) so we took any way which came first. There are a few streets, but the place is very small. There is a "High Street" and a "Dark Lane" – a jail half pulled down, a square tower in the centre of one of the streets, enclosed in an iron railing where we saw a chap lying drunk – any amount of "Grey Bull" Inns, and "Red Cows" etc., a policeman, a number of loafers and a pump without water. The first impressions we got of this great city were not the best. We were the centre of attraction for the natives whom I think we "astonished". After some trouble, and after asking some dozen or two people the way to the Bothwell Woods (being in blissful ignorance of the fact that the others were not there). We at length crossed another rickety bridge, walked up hill, passing, or rather stopping at, a seat, on the way. Here we left the initials "L. P." on its framework, together with some shavings, and after the ladies accompanying yours truly had arranged their headgear for the fifteenth time (less or more) we proceeded on our way to find the Bluebell woods leading to the Bothwell woods.

We found it indeed; we found the blue bells and found ourselves also in some private grounds from whence we were courteously expelled by the Gentleman in charge, who very thoughtfully shewed us the way to the Bothwell woods. It was four o'clock when we did get into these celebrated woods, but they were as deserted of human beings as the North Pole. So we resolved to go no further but to have something to eat, notwithstanding the very solemn but nonetheless painfully true fact that we had nothing with which to wash down the cakes and sandwiches. However we made ourselves happy and comfortable and, disregarding the fall of rain outside, as we were completely sheltered under the trees, we spread Liz's mackintosh and made the best of our opportunities – and space. Liz and I were huddled up, it is true. Feeling very thirsty indeed, we returned to the town and went into the Cocoa Rooms, where we enjoyed ourselves by smiling violently at the glasses etc. on the table. We tramped about the town a bit and then returned to the woods, eating Voses toffee the while. We sat on the seat until after 8, when returning to the Station we fell in with Dan and Arthur and the other fellow. We had a long wait for the train which was $1/4$ of an hour late. Until 10 o'clock the Garthwaite party sang after the Salvation Army style, namely, on the platform, with action movements and drill.

There was a rush for the already filled carriages when the express arrived "puffin' and blawin' as tho' it had been runnin' aal the way!" We had almost despaired of getting seated at all, when the Guard unlocked a door (as they had to do at the Central this morning) and we got in. But alas, not alone! Not even alone with Dan and Arthur and company, but five other gentlemen of ungentlemanly demeanour seated themselves next us. They were half-decent chaps though and might have been much worse; but, oh, the noise they made! They shrieked and howled at the windows in a lingering and hair raising farewell to Morpeth, and made the air hideous with their din, after which they calmly shut the windows and proceeded to smoke us out. But they were courteous enough to open them a little way at our request. But no sooner was the train under way and the evil of smoking (!) gave place to singing – and such singing. Two of their number were armed with Stentor-like voices, but the sounds proceeding from the throats of aforementioned gentlemen were very far from melodious. Liz was rather quiet and Jenny on the opposite side tried to look composed although her face belied her feelings in its color. And so after all, we didn't get a carriage to ourselves – didn't even go through a tunnel, when we should have hoped a long journey. But now we were glad to get out into the open air.

Liz and Jen and I, and the other 3 lads from Dunston, got out together and Jen left us at the Central Station portico. Liz and I came home guided by the Trio just mentioned; they disappeared, or rather dropped in the rear on the Gateshead side. I got some books at Birkets, and then Liz and I came home together when I kissed her and said "Good Night."

May 27th.(Sun.) [1894]

They would not believe <u>here</u> that it was so fine at Morpeth yesterday. It rained "cats and dogs" this morning here. I have no doubt but that 'twill be fine over yonder, but I have no wish to be there. I have had enough and to spare of Morpeth for some time.

May 30th. (Wed.) [1894]

Sunny morning until 11. Rained in torrents during dinner hour. Queer weather? Rather! Minnie brought up my tea to work as usual and I got home after 8! I did not see Liz until 5 to 9! What a shame! I think <u>she</u> thought; I believe she felt rather hurt, poor bairn, but I really couldn't get sooner.

June 1st. (Fri.)

The April invoices are packed out today and we commence May

work. I was late in getting up the lane where I saw Liz – a long way up – just a bit before 9. It was 10 past 10 when we got "hyem".

June 4th. (Mon.) [1894]

This has been a remarkable sort of day; not in the fact that it has been pouring rain nearly all day – that is nothing strange nowadays – but because I stayed indoors tonight! Yes! It really came to pass. At 9-30, however, I varied the night's proceedings by going out in the rain armed with the following warlike weapons: a hammer, a screwdriver, a notice bill, and a box of tacks. When my operations were completed the notice ran as follows:

JUVENILE MISSIONARY MEETING Sunday June 10 at 6pm,

Addresses by Messrs. Andrew T Hopper, and John Taylor (!), Recitations – Special Anthems by the choir (pronounced "Quihr"). The sole spectators of my antics in attaching to the notice-board the above startling announcement were Messrs Wm. Maddock and Ben Thompson – who viewed the proceedings with stoical and unchristian (very unchristian for they would not help a bit!) composure.

June 10th. (Sun.) [1894]

6 o'clock soon came and I was in the pulpit, "Organ to the right of me; Chairman to the left of me, audience in front of me gaped there, and wondered."

Mr. Davis Smith took the chair and read a speech on his own account after which the choir sang an anthem; then Miss Agnes Sharp recited. She was followed by your humble servant who forthwith proceeded with parched lips to give out the hymn. I immediately began to be shaky but got the better of it after I had proceeded with my paper. I warmed into the thing as I went on and ended in a very triumphant manner, then sat down.

Mr Andrew T. Hopper's address was good, but for his ungrammatical and highly pitched language. Lily T. recited and the choir sang a second anthem. Then the band – no! – the organ played, and we all came out.

It was still raining! How vexatious. I am glad Liz liked my paper; it is gratifying to know that she liked it._ We couldn't go for a walk to night, so Liz went with Jen to the latter's house and I wended my weary way homewards. I felt decidedly damp in every sense of the term. I have been awfully sleepy tonight through not being out. It is dreadfully close.

June 18th. (Mon.) [1894]

I must confess I am getting weary of writing in this book day after day; it is too monotonous, and I don't know why I do write, after all. Excessively hot weather. After I had returned tonight from my usual ramble, I lined in "Canova's Lion." I am rather puzzled now how to get models. I'm afraid I'll not get on well. It is another ambitious subject.

June 21st. (Thurs.) [1894]

This has been a lovely day and no mistake. (Stiflingly hot and not a breath of air or a drop of rain.) I am trying to get out the invoices before the race holidays, but Mr D. isn't helping me. He interrupts the work with other less important. We only got 2 days holiday last year. I trust we will get more this time. Race week next week The School breaks up today for a month's vacation. Liz P. is in ecstasies, although she denies it. She says to me every minute: "A Month's holiday, John hinny!" and so on and so on. I did not work long tonight. Stan and I are heartily tired of this overtime work; it is paying but not for the health I'm afraid.

June 22nd. (Fri.) [1894]

As per usual. (Only I got 3 Kisses instead of one.)

July 1st. (Sun.) [1894]

This is a splendid and glorious day. It is 12 o'clock. Liz has just passed the window in white waist and blue skirt. (She didn't look across though.)

July 2nd. (Mon.) [1894]

The weather was simply delicious. I got round at 7 and "What a scene was there". Murphy with his roundabouts (Horses and Gondola's) had, of course, the monopoly. There was a tremendous crush all night and well on to morning. Plenty of shooting galleries but not much else. The roundabouts are lit by electricity, and every part is beautifully gilded and ornamented in the most tasteful and artistic manner. It was just like a fairy scene but for the absence of the fairies and the presence of many blackguards and dreadful organs.

Liz and Jen1 were together all the night. Liz and Jen and I were on the horses and in the cars for some time; these things sicken me but Liz enjoys them. She was in half a dozen times before I came.

July 16th. (Mon.) [1894]

M. N C. Annual Trip to Tynemouth. Of course it rained! What else could be expected? _ And St. Swithin's weather too. Six weeks of it – ugh! I went to work carrying thereto the results of my labour. Mr D. seemed surprised when I intimated my desire to go. However, in spite of protestations from all at home, I went by the 12-30 boat. (Mr D. went by ditto. boat.) to Newcastle. I met Will Maddock in the Central Station and we went down together in the 5 past 1 train. The rain ceased at midday, and we never felt a drop until the next day, although of course it was not fine; cloudy but warm enough. The Ferry Co. got pay from the children and did not charge any fee as has usually been the case. Two boats left the landing here, but the people were removed all into one at the Quayside, from whence she proceeded on her journey. It did not rain much until the passengers were landed, but then – oh! – Liz and Miss S. (Jen 2) with her friend Miss Bella Kirton went by boat. I saw them at 9 o'clock when I was going up to D. E. W. Liz tells me that the rain was simply dreadful all the morning, but the principal woe of these three poor maidens was the fact that they went into a cocoa room and could only obtain sandwiches covered with mustard and none without. Liz and her friends were at the Station to meet us. Will M. lost his stick in the train. We came down onto the sands, where W. M. told Ada I "set" them away and went with him until tea time. Well not exactly; they, Liz etc., were discreet enough to see that I couldn't go about with three girls all the afternoon. They went and had their photos taken, and "guys" they were. All the faces were as though they had been shot at with grape – honeycombed & perforated. Some of us went out in a boat

July 20th. (Fri.) [1894]

Sultry all day; raining this morning. It is striking midnight while I write but I will go on till I finish for this day. I am happy and yet unsatisfied. I have been at School of Art tonight and – but soft! I must go my usual road after the orthodox fashion. Did not work overtime.

I went up Gateshead at 7 o'clock, to the School of Art and found Mr White gazing in a puzzled manner over the first results of the exam. He was delighted to shew me an "Ex" after my name opposite "Antique" which contrasted strangely with the _ (Failure) for "Life Drawing." I regret the __ very much, I did not expect such a poor result; "try again" of course! I have scored a first for Clay Modelling.

Here are the results as far as I am concerned:

Clay Modelling FIRST   Life Fail   Antique Ex.

Kettlewell has only got a second in Clay Modelling for which he expected better; but on the contrary he has secured a First for "Life". (I am delighted to know this – K. is a genius!) Mr Wild has once more got a second for "Life"; only he and K are named as having passed at all. There were three of us in for Antique and this is the result (Tourtel and Fearon have both sat before for same): Tourtel, Second; Fearon, Second; Taylor, (as above) Altogether it is a most surprising result. They are sad, lots of those who gazed ruefully at that fatal paper. But the results, as a whole, are good. We amused ourselves for the rest of the night. There were a few sketches, but not many "Tuppences" given out. This is the breaking up night at the school. Holiday for 2 months.

Liz was at the end of Swinburne St. and we went home together. Liz looked so bonny and tempting tonight. Her great eyes were flashing and brilliant, and her lips were rosy red; I won't see her till Sunday, mind, and yet I couldn't get a kiss at all at all! Because some women were talking half a mile away! Pity! Pity isn't the word for it. She told me to practice on Minnie for one night. But I haven't. I'll just kiss my hand, fancy it is my dear lass, and go to bed content. Just half past twelve!.

July 21st. (Sat.)

I did what may safely and certainly be termed a "daft" trick this morning in getting on to the landing without the money bag. I had to jump aboard again and go to Elswick and back for my foolishness. Mr D. didn't say anything although I was $^1/_4$ hour late.

AH and his stick! (What helps me on my weary way? What keeps the howling curs at bay? My stick!)

Sun 22nd. July [1894]

I am dying for a – a – stick! (Andrew has got one _ can't come out without it now!) And I must needs have one too. I told Liz that AH had his stick, but I knew where to put my hands – but only when she was with me. I don't know what to do with them when I am alone or with her in company. I must have a stick – so I cut one from a tree for the time being. (I think Tom and Edward are going to London (Rly. Trip) about the middle of August. I believe I shall be asked too.) This looks well!

But I have had to make the best of it!! It was a blot! Not a tear. Liz is so queer and so nice! We came through by the fields and we two went by the school's way. As it was only about 9-30 we decided to wander Hopper's field until 10. However, we were "frightened away by two horses who didn't want our company".

July 29th. (Sun.) [1894]

Miss C. Taylor and a Miss Robinson were here to tea. Splendid weather. I tried to haul AH up tonight but he wasn't "having any" – neither was Sallie (H), poor soul! He had to fall back on Geo W. Liz and I went the same road as yesternight, where we met millions of people much to my annoyance – inwardly – among the lot of whom we met was Mr. & Mrs. White (of School Of Art fame). We spoke – I didn't blush – and passed on. It is a lovely walk – but for the people.

August 2nd. (Thurs.) [1894]

I went up the lane and waited for Liz. We sat down in the shadows of the "Wonderful Forest" and stayed there until dusk. Liz is all right again.

August 4th. (Sat.) [1894]

We are to have holiday – whole day on Monday first (Bank Holiday.) I went to Newcastle, and, among other things bought colors and yellow shoes and stick. (I am turning dreadfully "stuck up".)

Later on Liz and I found ourselves together, leaning against the wood railings of the "Forest". Here we stayed until the "hour for parting" drew nigh. Liz has taken a fancy to my stick and its smell has tickled her nostrils.

August 6th. (Mon.) [1894]
(A whole Holiday!) Liz and I went for a walk, of course.
August 11th, (Sat.) [1894]
<u>Choir Trip to Linty Green (Chopwell Woods)</u>.

It proved fine until the afternoon when in spite of an occasionally dazzling sun the rain often came down in drenching showers. The notice read to the effect that we were to leave chapel at 2 as the train at Swalwell was 2-39. There was a good turn up – perhaps over thirty. 2 o'clock was late enough but 10 past 2 was out of all question too late in starting. They were saying in going up "Why are you in such a hurry? There's plenty of time!" Well, a few of us got into Swallwell in advance of the others when it began to rain heavily, and so long did it continue that we were forced to take shelter. After being drenched through we hurried to the station (being the second instalment), and got there just in time to see the train leaving! This was at 2-49 (10 minutes later than the notice said) and the next was not until 4-15, $1\frac{1}{2}$ hours we had to wait for the next train! The ladies all arrived by 3-30 anyway so that wasn't so bad. We amused ourselves as best we could during the rather long interval – reading, eating, singing, playing concertina, duck stone, gathering flowers, kicking up shindigs etc. etc. We were glad enough when the train rushed in and when we <u>ourselves</u> were rushed <u>therein</u>. Even before they had got out of the train, some of these Choir gentlemen shewed themselves very shabby. I had plenty of proof before the day was out. We all got out at Linty Green and commenced the pilgrimage. It had been fair whilst we were in the train, but the rain commenced when we had gone only a short way towards the woods. When we got fairly under the shelter of the trees it came down very <u>wet</u> and very heavily. Liz and I (of course <u>Liz</u> was there, AH or AB weren't) and Ben and Bella lagged behind and sat down for better shelter. The advance guard struggled on and succeeded in finding in finding the hospitable farmhouse where 'twas arranged we should have our teas. We four arrived a few minutes after the rest, and found the table was being sumptuously set for tea. (It was, of course, too damp to have tea outside as had been at first arranged). There were plates and dishes of cakes and breads innumerable, and there was any amount of stuff left after everybody had finished. (Some of those shabby chaps again made holes in their manners – they can't help it – "what's bred in the bone" etc.) But everybody was very happy. After tea we "<u>went for</u>" the swings – <u>such</u> swings, and there were two of 'em.

Hall took a group for a photograph (it turned out a splendid photo, best of the sort I have seen) and then we played several games in the fields. Before we came away, I helped Liz to enjoy herself on the swing. Tom Birtley had been "swinging her before". He was a beautiful "pusher" (i.e. pusher of swing) she said so I mush redeem my honor and retrieve my fallen fortunes! I did at least she said so. Last thanks we gave to the people were the singing of two pieces, "Song of Hope" and "Phyllis". The Choir sang whilst a few of us washed our hands and faces round at the other side of the house. The walk back to the Station was very pleasant. 'Twas eleven o'clock before we got home, having spent one of the pleasantest days we could remember.

August 14th. (Tues.) [1894]

Oh! Dear, dear!! This awful overtime. I couldn't get out till nearly 8-30; I went across to No 14 to tell Liz, who wasn't expecting me till 9; I almost hoped she would haul me inside; I <u>should</u> like to have a night beside the dear girl in her own house; but my hopes (?) were dashed when she said "What a <u>beautiful</u> night." (The moon was struggling with monstrous black rain clouds; it had been raining nearly all day.) I went on in front and waited until Liz arrived. I waited at" the Tree". It is such a fine old tree growing where the two main roads join. Best of all for our purpose, it serves as a seat for there is a great branch running for some feet almost parallel with the ground and only four feet above it. On this, close to the great trunk, which covers up 2 persons quite easily, we rest; I sit and Liz stands, but when 'tis over light to be observed she has sat also.

August 15th. (Wed.) [1894]

(I think we ought to have a timetable for ourselves. First question when we arrive at our rendezvous at 10 o'clock is "Where are we going tomorrow night?") We went up Havis's Bank and found another place at the top of the field, beside <u>new</u> "forest". There is a magnificent moon; it is rather bright though; we like cloudy nights.

August 16th. (Thu.) [1894]
The results of Higher Grade School Exams are in the Chronicle tonight. Liz has come off badly as she expected. The lottery is viz:–
Mathematics: Jen S., Pass; Liz P. Fair.
Freehand & Model: Jen, 2 nd in both. Liz, Nil.
I learn that there have been many opinions given. Liz says Jen. S. is amazed that she (Liz) has not got even second, and is sorry as a friend always is. Jen L. has not offered any remarks that have been heard but I suspect she will not be vexed (I am not spiteful.) Jen L. will take Miss Hunter's views, namely: that Liz ought not to keep company with a lad during her apprenticeship, as it hinders her from doing her lessons properly. She ought only to take half an hour's recreation, alone! (Perhaps there is a little something in the first bit, but certainly Liz attended well to all her lessons, at school at day and at school at night.) Miss H. cannot say that she has not worked hard. Ada has not said much; she is very sorry, but does not blame Liz at all. Liz had not a proper teacher anyway. Lil said: "You know I'd like you to pass, Liz, but I hope you don't," because she wanted to go to her class next year.

Liz herself is sorry about the results, and somewhat surprised; anybody who didn't know her might say she doesn't care, judging from appearances, but that is absurd. Poor Liz was sure to feel disappointed, and I know that she will feel it. Liz and I went along the beaten track of a certain field and sat down, and well! She forgot all about the exam in her merriment when coming home.

August 17th. (Fri.) [1894] The days are fine but occasionally it rains deluges. Liz was so miserable this morning at school, with Miss H's preaching, that she told me she didn't want to go back in the afternoon. She wrote a note to me and asked me to reply, which I did. We two went along by the Forge tonight and stayed beside the Tree.

August 18th. (Sat.) [1894]
I was up at 6-30 this morning, and had as the "BOP" calls it the morning tub. I wrote in this book until 8, and went to Newcastle at 8-30 for the wages as usual.

The exhibits were rather good (according to the verdict of the knowing ones) and not so good as last year but better then Gateshead.

The prizes were shockingly paltry. (I don't include <u>my sketch</u>, of course!! It was "won" by some people of the High End called Arkless, but curiously it goes into the same house as my other one - the Four Lane Ends, painted for the Flower Show last year.)

The field (Garbutt's) presented a very lively sight; people of all sorts and conditions (looking to a "dressy" point of view, but excluding princes of the blood), were to be found: young, old and middle aged; well-off folk and poor people and poorer; vagabonds and rogues and Christians rubbed shoulders; the Gods predominating. We came home at 10.

August 25th. (Sat.) [1894]

Liz P. went down and came back in same boat. I forgot my promise to be out at 7-30 and had to rush out at ? to 8. I soon found my love at Havis's stile, then I made a fool of myself and we went further up. I was trying to convince Liz that sight travelled faster than sound.

They are having great demonstrations over Elswick way.

Circuses etc. and performing acrobats. Balloons ascend every night and they charge to go up. Besides there are parachutists – a man and girl. I saw one of 'em up tonight. I think it was the man. There was a lovely sunset and the whole of the sky in that quarter was flooded with grey and gold with a crimson haze softening the whole.

The <u>Balloon</u> ascended to a great altitude, so high that it looked only a big as a shilling and 'twas difficult to see any part of the car or parachute – then became seemingly stationary. We watched eagerly with all our eyes, as did no doubt thousands of others, and waited expectantly. Suddenly a speck, or rather a line, shot like one of Jove's arrows from the unobscured heavens. It seemed a long time before the parachute began to open, which it did suddenly and in an instant the rapid progress was checked and the thing floated gently and calmly downwards like a big straw hat, though of course it kept its equilibrium, and came down and down till it was lost from our view on the line of sight.

Some minutes later the balloon which apparently had not risen higher, shewed by its baggy appearance that the gas was rapidly escaping. Presently it seemed to wither up and came down somewhat faster than the parachute, but looking like a wobbly exclamation stop or a note of interrogation.

Now I have got out of my latitude (but I suppose I must "show off" – can't help it!). Liz and I were as "kiss and kind" as could be. We went a long way up; it was very dark indeed. A shabby old bit of a crescent moon "glowered for a bit, cut into several pieces by strips of cloud, and then was swallowed up in darkness." We sat down for a few minutes & I smoked. Then Liz drew me back home. We stood a good bit at the "C. door". W. Golightly has gone for 3 years but Liz couldn't let me. away for 3 weeks. She wouldn't let me go up in a balloon for a few minutes for fear of accidents – and yet she said tonight – because (quoting a paper), when the lad kisses the girl, it is not the aforementioned's wish, but the desire thus conveyed from the girl, impels the lad to give her the desired kiss __ well because I believe (?) in this, and I said 'twas her (Liz) that desired me to kiss her. She said there wouldn't be any more kissing and she wouldn't kiss me any more. So I came away – at 10 o'clock.

Sept. 1st. (Sat.) [1894]

"Immersion at 6!" Am going to Haydon Bridge this afternoon. Arrived at Gateshead High end at 1, so as I had some time to spare I went up to the Library, hoping to find more Exam Results. My hopes were not dashed – at least so far as the fact of the results being out because mine are not particularly brilliant. This is how it has come out along with those, see July 20th.

More	Life Fail	Clay Modelling 1 st .
Exam	Principles of O. Fail	Shading Model 1 st
Results.	Perspective 2nd.	Ornament Cast. 1 st .

Antique ex. and the "Antinous" (outline) accepted.

I am sorry about the perspective and P. of Ornament. Mr Wilkinson taught both but if I am thick at those subjects it isn't his fault. I did my best and expected better results.

HAYDON BRIDGE (Flower Show) I rushed off to the train at $1/4$ past 1 and got into the wrong station. When I had righted myself, Ed came in, just as the train was ready to leave. We got in. Mater and Lily, with Mr and Mrs .Hall had already embarked. It is a very pleasant journey up to Haydon Bridge and the day was beautifully fine. Lots of people got out at Prudhoe where there was a Flower Show. We found that a Miss P. was waiting at the station. Ed. introduced us. She is rather pretty and dark, but talks somewhat roughly. She took us up to their house where we were introduced to all the folks, and a swarm of them there are. They seem always to have people staying with them. We found their food, meat, butter, milk etc. to be much superior to that used here at Dunston.

I forgot at the time the Diary, and have lost the particulars of the things. We travelled a good deal. There was a flower show to which we all went. Cousin Lizzie and another friend of hers, also a Lizzie (nice name Lizzie!) the last but one a nice little girl enough, very jolly and good natured. It was pouring rain outside the tents all the time, so we travelled round and round the show. The two Lizzies were full of fun and mischief. They ransacked my pockets and little Lizzie got possession of my little diminishing glass which I have had so long. I was rather sorry at this, not of course for its value (I bought it for a very small sum!) although it always was a very useful little friend when I was painting – but more because of its associations. They also saw my old "bad tempered" portrait and wanted to keep it, but I promised to send Cousin Lizzie one of the other ones, and she returned the old photo, promising to return the glass next time I went to stay, (I intend to go for a week, in a short time when I get my holidays) and in the meantime I had to send a photo.

Sept. 2nd. (Sun.) [1894]
HAYDON BRIDGE Sunday School ANNIVERSARY.

I guess most of the merry makers felt unhappy this morning after last night's "jollification". After breakfast we went out for a walk on the hills amongst the stubby grass and bushy braes, and new nuts. It was cool enough but the air is bracing and invigorating. There was a tremendous feast at one o'clock. I was rather tired of their talk; they can't talk common sense much less decency; of course there must be allowance made, they see few people but those of their own stamp.

In the afternoon we went to Langley Castle, a few miles away. The old stone work is splendid and the new is also excellent. After we had gone through passages and labyrinths innumerable, and passed niches and windows and pits and trapfalls innumerable without number, some of the passages of which had winding stairs where only one thin person at a time could ascend, we got unto the roof. There was a rather laughable incident there. Some visitors, ladies and gentlemen, wished to go down and one of the men in advance, expecting all of us had got up, went down – but getting halfway, found two or three people ascending and had to beat a retreat to the top again. He waited for some minutes and then again expecting the coast to be clear made a second attempt, to be only again disappointed. The third attempt was more successful. We had a magnificent view of the surrounding country, from our great altitude. We looked out from the niches and towers and bastions, frightening to death an old man far below in a garden, who was watching us. The great walls of the castle are <u>seven</u> feet thick and the towers will be 100 feet high, which gives it a very imposing appearance. The whole of one side is covered with evergreens. We came back slowly.

DROWNED IN THE RIVER. E. Simpson

A very sad and lamentable accident occurred here tonight at 8 o'clock. A young lad and two girls, all belonging to the village were getting into a small boat at Dunston landing; the unfortunate one being in, and her friend in the act of getting in beside her. The latter slipped and clutched at the others with the result that she herself was saved but dragged the others into the water. The lad did his best no doubt, but one of the poor girls sank almost immediately, and was drowned. Her body was not recovered until late at night. Her name is <u>Elizabeth Simpson, aged 17</u>.

September 4th. (Tues.) [1894]

Posted today a photo of mine to Miss Elizabeth Pickering.

(I couldn't get out of this mess; it was a compromise!)

Liz and I went for a walk after which it rained a bit.

September 9th. (Sun) [1894]

I wasn't at Chapel this morning but I suppose it was <u>good</u>. Ogden was preaching. Liz was at Newcastle today, at Sunday School where attend Miss. S. and her friend Miss. Kirton of whom I have spoken before. She liked it very much. We went for a walk by Nanny's Wood.

I like to see Liz with her hair fastened at the back with ribbon, it suits her more. Her face looks very clear and pale in the moonlight and her eyes shine dark with remarkable lustre. Liz's waist is same as ever and she is very pliable and "giving", dear child. I can do as I wish now; she is so loving and so nice that I imagine all sorts of good things. I like to kiss her sweet face and long for a kiss from her own red lips. I think she sighs for me at 10 o'clock! Got back my watch at last!

September 12th. (Wed.) [1894]

Worked overtime and then went for a walk with my dearly beloved.

October 1 st (Mon.) [1894]

It is of no use trying to distinguish one day from another. I can't write in here every day for I have other duties to perform __ and yet I feel for my old habit of writing in the diary. I would miss it very much, although I have two others before this – but never mind; I need not put down every day particularly from the other when there is nothing particularly striking to relate. Monday, class; Tuesday, class; Thursday, Anatomy & Architecture class; Friday, class – with letters in between, very thickly interspersed. Liz wrote me a very beautiful letter on 1 st , bits of which I cannot, for love & pride, refrain from quoting: "Dear John, Are you vexed at this last change?" (It is in connection with a religious idea; of course I am not vexed!) "I feel as I never felt before, the responsibility of my influence." ... "Although the future is so dark I seem to have faith and live in the present. I must seem strange to you for I feel I am not like other girls of my age and yet I for myself would not be otherwise. Sometimes I think you must be weary of my religious views but I can't help them, they are now part of my life and it is such a comfort to know that all is for the best when I think of the troubles of our family which I would always be fretting over if I had to bear them alone."

Liz has, I may say, very good and practical views of religion & I like her to talk on this strain, as she often does. In an earlier part of this letter she had talked about confiding in AH if ever we two (Liz and I) fell out about anything. I said in the reply: "I am glad you said that about your thinking you should confide in Andrew H. if ever we were in trouble. I would wait patiently for years for you and your love. I can never forget your teaching, and, above all, your example. I think contact with you has improved me greatly. I feel quite different in mind from what I was a year or so ago. You have taught me by word and by deed, and I thank God that ever we were brought together, even though it is not to be for always. Dear Liz, accept the thanks which I cannot speak to you, and may I never forget it. Your ever loving friend."

    October 6th. (Sat.) [1894]

    I went to Newcastle this afternoon at 2-30 and did not get back till __, well look here. I got the frames, after I had had a walk round the town, and they were a weight and went by tram to Elswick Library. I left the frames in the passage and went to get a book. If the lad hadn't taken so long to get the book I wanted (Charles Reeve's "<u>Wandering Heir</u>"), I might have caught the boat. I got the book, snatched up the frames, and ran for the landing at break-neck pace, and at the risk of dislocating my ankle or shoulder, and was just in time to see the boat leaving! __ I wasn't "like a lamb" at that moment. I was subdued enough however, when I left my frames at the landing and sauntered back in the rain too! – to the library, where I read until next boat time. Got aboard all safe, frames and all went down cabin to read. Got off at Dunston landing, all safe, book in hand, went up bridge – Left frames!

    Rushed back into the boat like a rocket! Yelled to the boat men to stop; they smiled like the torturers of the Inquisition and the wheels went round all the faster. I had wild notions of jumping overboard and swimming with the frames to land; but the water would have been cold, and it was raining too. And I was going to Newcastle all the time! Had had no tea! Had lost the boat once and was clinging to it to make up second time! Off to Quayside again for an hours trip more, and Liz was waiting of me; and it was $\frac{1}{2}$ past 7 now!!! I <u>was</u> like a lamb then!!!! Ah! Laugh you may. It is a humiliating incident to bring back to a proud and wounded heart! I did not forget the frames this next time! I got in beside Liz at 8-30 and was happy then! I told her of my sufferings!! And it was ten o'clock before she'd let me go.

    October 11th. (Thurs.) [1894]

    Architecture and Anatomy. This last subject delights me. Mr White takes the class.

October 12th. (Fri.) [1894]

Liz and co. are preparing for the <u>Exam tomorrow</u>. I did not go to class tonight. I went and sought Liz and we went for a walk in the moonlight. Of course I wished her success for tomorrow's ordeal.

October 13th. (Sat.) [1894]

The following ladies were examined at Jarrow by H. M. Inspectors today, from 9-30 till 5-30 in the 3 R's and many more. Miss P. and Miss Satchwell, 3 rd year; Lily T. and Georgina Buckton, first years. I hope they have all done well. Ada was down with them. Ada and Co. came back (wet though) about ½ past 6. I went to see Liz at 8 o'clock. It was raining a good excuse for an "At Home". We decided to have one. And it was a thorough success; haven't time to say more, except that 10 o'clock came all too soon.

October 16th. (Tues.) [1894]

Did modelling at Venus head. Came down with Kettlewell, who understands.

October 17th. (Wed.) [1894]

I suppose there must have been an "At Home" tonight.

October 18th. (Thurs.) [1894]

Mr. White was absent, ill, tonight. We sketched a human skull instead.

October 24th. (Wed.) [1894]

Of course I went across tonight to my guardian angel and couldn't be parted from her until the usual hour of ten.

October 26th. (Fri.) [1894]

Office Grievances There was an awful row up at D. E. W. this morning. Mr Armstrong thinks that we are not working hard enough, or <u>fast</u> enough. Here is our case, stated in black and white, and without exaggerating in the least, or fancying ourselves martyrs.

At the commencement of the year, the old system of book keeping was abandoned, and Mr Armstrong started a new one. We were six weeks late in starting, and being new to the work, didn't get on as fast as Mr A. seemed to like. Well, we didn't gain as time went on, as there was plenty of work for us all to do. Shortly after, to make matters better, Mr A. found excuse to send off Rowat, and Stanley and I had virtually to do our own and his amongst us. There was now an enormous amount of work to do and we have never made any headway since; in fact, although we have stayed overtime for months, day after day almost, we can't keep up. Now it is quite plain that someone else will have to help us. F. W. W. might work harder; and Mr D. might do a little work, of any kind, or at least not interrupt so much. Now Mr A. refuses to get anyone else, and wishes us to work overtime always, it would seem. But I for myself don't intend to work overtime any longer if it can be helped.

Well, Mr A. got onto our bones this morning. He didn't say much to me but opened out like a fury on Stanley who works with F. W. W. upstairs. He had told S. to work overtime, but didn't mention any period of time, as he said (a fortnight) to me. He was going to play H_l with us, if Mr Fairley (Colliery Manager) blamed him for not sending the invoices sooner, and in any case, is going to be straight by not paying is a d — -d ha'penny for overtime we have already worked (the fortnight). I think this is shameful! I saw Mr D. but he said he would see that we were paid for all we worked. I am sick of this, and was in two minds about giving my notice then and there; I am utterly miserable when working overtime. Stanley is going to apply for the first decent advert for clerk, which he sees. I don't know how 'twill end. We both stayed overtime tonight until 8-30. At 9 I went to Liz's and cuddled her till 10 o'clock. I had written a long letter to Liz about all my (above) troubles.

October 27th. (Sat.) [1894]
Great Choral Contest at the Olympia.

M. N. C. choir in the swim. Dunston turned out today her choicest. The Choir went forth in the old style, ignoring rain and mud and false prophets. (No! I fancy Biblical language will have a better effect.)

And behold the people heard and there was great wonderment throughout the city (i.e. Dunston), for there were many who spoke ill of the Master (i.e. Jack Noble) and his disciples (i.e. the Choir.); moreover great multitudes followed him, even across the Jordan, (ie. Tyne.) Unto the place set apart for the ~SONGS of Gladness. And when they were set the multitudes from afar off came unto the Place, which is called unto this day, Olympia. And after all things were ready, behold a man arrayed in robes of state entered into the Judges abode, whither he stirred not nor opened not his mouth until all the people had sent forth their songs unto the ears of the multitude. And this is the order in which the choirs sang their praises, the Judge where of saw not, neither knew he them; moreover the Judge yet listeneth & heareth and maketh many wise and otherwise predictions, whereat many murmured against him. Nevertheless, before these things came to pass, behold, while we yet looked, lo! They came forth in battle array:

1. South Bank (Evans)   "How Sweet the moonlight sleeps"
2. Dunston (Noble)   " Break the cold grey stones"
3. Teesside (Nichol)   "Let the hills resound with song"
4. Shields (Dockseys)   "Excelsior"
5. Southbank Baptist (Davis) "O Gladsome Light"
6. Spennymoor (Ward)   "Heavenly War" (best)
7. Spennymoor (Roberts)   "Our Father" (worst)
8. Cramlington   "Awake Eolian Lyre.

And the people paid heed unto the singing and were exceeding glad. And when the South Bank Choir had sung and the multitude were exceeding glad, behold they clapped their hands and shouted exceedingly. And when the Dunston Choir had rendered, behold! the room was filled with the noise of many voices & with the sounds of clapping of hands. And the leader of the singers from Dunston was called John son of Matthew(Noble) And John son of Matthew was exceeding glad after the song had been sung and waxed merry. And behold! one Macintyre, and one Thwaites, prophets in the land of the Gut, prophesied, whereat the people were astonished; moreover they felt glad exceedingly. For they said "And the second shall be first; take ye heed." And other choirs sang and the great building called Olympia was filled with all kinds of music. And some of the music was good, whereupon the multitude was attentive and many were the scribes that were there for they took note of the songs. And the song they sang was "Behold Mary! Go ye and call home the cattle, which feedeth by the stream of Dee." (O! Mary go and call the cattle home.) Moreover much of the singing was exceeding cruel (i.e. scandalous).

A voice came to Spennymoor which is in the county of Durham saying "Arise go forth to meet thy enemy," and behold, both leaders heard and went. And lo! They both came forth, one against another (and they both of them were Spennymoorites). And they sang, and the people murmured; and many clapped their hands and shouted in derision, whereupon the leader of one choir, which was a man strangely fashioned bowed low, whereat the hearts of the scoffers smote them, for they mocked. And when they had all sung their song, behold while we yet wondered, there was a great stir at the far end of the building and a multitude of singers began to gather upon one spot. And when all was set, lo! There came forth from the box wherein he had sat, the Judge, clothed in scarlet and fine linen, and mounted the seats upon the platform. Then there came forth from the mouths of the people of the eight choirs a sound as of the roaring of the wind and sounds as of the lullaby of Gentle Zephyrs, and it was good. And after this had come to pass there was a mighty applause for the people were glad. Then the multitude dispersed and the Judge over all came forth.

And a great silence fell, they being impatient to hear the judgement. And the judge spoke and the multitude lent attentive ear. And lo! The result was thusly:-

1 st prize: £20, to be divided between Dunston & Southbank.

2 nd prize: 35, Teesside.

And when the Dunstonites heard the news, behold they shouted and clapped their hands and made the house ring with wild applause. Dunston was first and behold throughout the land of the Staithes was rejoicing and making merry in celebration of the great victory. And all rejoiced with exceeding great joy. Dunston sang beautifully, splendidly, and exactly as the copy was written. My Liz was there <u>with me</u> of course. We came home by ourselves at 10-30.

November 1st. (Thurs.) [1894]
Usual lessons in Architecture and Anatomy tonight.

November 2nd. (Fri.) [1894]
Attempted a design for heading of "The Artist", tonight at class.

November 4th. (Sun.) [1894]

Sunday School in the afternoon of course. Walk and then an "At Home" at night.

November 6th. (Tue.) [1894]

Modelling at Venus head.

November 8th. (Thu..) [1894]

Architecture and Anatomy, or "Archie Tector" and "Annie Tommy"

November 9th.(Fri.) [1894]

This is a nice night too, which I like.

When I can do "anything", I do designs. I try to make "nice girls" etc.

November 11th. (Sun.) [1894]

A Sunday like all other Sundays to me. A Sunday is a blessed rest when one has worked hard all the week at work one doesn't love. AH (!) (of all persons) went with Liz and me up the lane tonight.

November 14th. (Wed.) [1894]

How delightful a night is Wednesday night! Ah! The bliss of a certain short period before 10 o'clock is indescribably delightful.

November 15th. (Thu.) [1894]

There was a poor attendance at the Architecture class tonight. Anatomy is very interesting. Mr. White is good at this subject. Miss Swift always answers, that is all I can say!

November 16th. (Fri.) [1894]

"Do anything I please" night! Drew a nice girl, in clinging robes, for the "Artist", but won't do, I think. I came down with Kettlewell, I believe.

November 17th. (Sat.) [1894]

I modelled in clay this afternoon, after I had <u>wallowed</u> in clay, in the clay pond (I couldn't obtain the pipe clay.) A pair of legs thus and then draped them with red cloth.

November 27th. (Tue.) [1894]

I blush to say that I am 19 years old today. It is no use disguising both facts – one that I really am 19, and the other that I am terribly grieved about it. Liz wrote a note; I wrote a note; we each got one; the letter she got was dreary with dismal forbodings and looming terrors of old age, the other "O so bright" – cheerful and happy, and unworthy wretch that I am, she enclosed a birthday present in the shape of a pair of Sleeve links – such beautiful little things. I did not expect any gift, indeed I had no right to expect anything from my dear girl. I do not love her any more for the gift; I could not. I love her, "with a love" as the Arab says, "that will not die."

School of Art Social on Fri. Nov 29th.

Ada, Minnie and I went to the School and got there at 8 o'clock or thereabouts. The programme had commenced; an elderly lady in spectacles was singing. The concert was exceedingly good, especially in the comic and sentimental singers (rather queer bit this, but I refer to two in particular.) The refreshment room was opened after the programme of singing, and here Ada and Minnie became acquainted with all the great guns: Messrs. White, Wilkinson, Philipson, Wild etc. etc. Then The Thing of the Evening commenced – The Dance. I am not a judge of dancing; I am unable to dance – except perhaps to my own tunes, but I should like to be able to dance; my little sisters were so much delighted with the dance tonight that they promised to teach me before the quire (Choir, I mean). Social, promised on the spot. I watched the dancing and was delighted, even with watching "the mazy whirl". I thoro'ly enjoyed myself, and Ada and Minnie were in Ecstacies of delight, never enjoyed themselves more. I think everybody was happy that night and even now when its over, the recollection of the happy time is quite refreshing to think of. There were low- necked dresses and others (high necks I suppose) and all looked neat. Such a contrast, such harmonies of lovely tints and dazzling shades of colour – and pretty girls – looking bonny whether they were really bonny or plain. 'Tis always delightful to watch a company of ladies who are not too much affected (with pride) – a company of ladies, and well bred gentlemen.

December 1st.(Sat.) [1894]

The year is drawing to a close, another year, while yet the memories of last are scarcely yet gone from my mind. The year has sped at lightning speed apparently. I do not feel a year older and it is hard to believe that 'tis nigh on 12 months since we went out carol singing on Christmas Eve, and when I wrote long letters to my love who was gone from me.

December 8th. (Sat.) [1894]

The Presentation to Mr White.

There was a very good company, mostly the elders (like myself) or rather, all the quality – and yet <u>that</u> doesn't exactly explain what I intended to say – I was rather modest, but having given a little introduction I will say without apologising – er – all the clever folks – myself of course – I was there . Mr. Wilkinson made the presentation, halfway down the programme, with a very suitable speech, in which he, however, completely broke down.– his feelings seem to overcome him and it was really very touching. He said he divided Mr. White into 3 heads (there was laughter here), as a Manager who looked after and conducted all the thousand and one difficulties of the school, secondly he was a Teacher in which capacity he excelled – and in the third case as a Friend. A friend that spoke what he thought, a friend that told the truth and pointed out the faults and failings, as well as the good points.

He finished by saying that he had pleasure in making the presentation and hoped that so long as the lamp shed its brilliant rays and lighted Mr. White on his worldly way, so long would Mr. White's genial influence be to the students of the school, an example to copy from.

Mr. White said he was not cut out for speaking. He was grateful indeed for the splendid gift of which he said he was quite unworthy as he had always done only what he considered his duty towards the students, and nothing more. He would continue in the same way, to teach and not to flatter anyone. (Mr. White always <u>was</u> that way.) He never put on any sham. He always ran at a regular pace for exams, throughout the year; in the other way he was just the same. He told the students their good points; he told them their bad points too, but that was only what he considered right. For the reason of receiving this splendid gift, he would not change his ways with the students; he would be the same honest critic; he would still be the fault finder and everything with him, would go on as usual. (Mr W. went on in this strain for some time, shewing out in true colours the character of the man, as we all know him, and said a good deal more, making a very fair speech, which was warmly applauded.)

The programme was especially good. Miss Swift sang, Mr Stevenson played the pianoforte Miss Marsh did ditto, Mr. Wild sang (capitally) two songs; Mr. Pearson sang very well too; and so did Mr. Geo Young – and Miss Wild. The affair wound up at 9 o'clock and I rushed home to see my love, my Liz for $\frac{1}{2}$ hr.

December 24th. (Mon.) [1894] Xmas Eve

We were off today. I went to Grainger St, Newcastle. I saw Liz and Jen Satchwell on my way – the latter I had seen at 9-15 when I went to Elswick, and I thought she didn't speak to me, but she did it appears. I thought she looked very pretty this morning; she had a rosy colour in her cheeks. They spoke a few words and I went on my way. I bought some Xmas cards. Liz and I went for a walk, I think, and then I went across till 10. When I came home there were an assembly of people, a Mr & 2 Misses Maddocks. At 11-35 they all went down to the Chapel – Liz and I followed , shortly before 12.

December 25th. (Tue.) [1894] Xmas Morning

Christmas day dawned and found us (not freezing – not at all! – but sweating with the tremendous heat) as we plodded our way up Gateshead after the choir people who were courteous enough to hurry off without us. We found 'em high up Gateshead, and met them coming in an opposite direction; both parties landing at Maddock's door.

We sang and then all hands (camp followers included) piped to supper. It was an hour later, two o'clock, before we got away. We sang at a few houses in Gateshead and then came down to Dunston. I want to hear "Christians awake", "Jesus shall reign" and "Rock of Ages" no more till next Xmas morning. We were well nigh tired out when we sang at our house, where we stayed and ate nuts for some time, and then decamped. Tired here at no. 23 but we were by no means finished. We were done up (for singing but not for <u>eating</u>) when we got to Mrs. Hopper's where we did full justice to the feast. The P. C. (Lawson, who by the way, sang a song in our house) did to the supper, <u>more</u> than full justice. (Liz and I lost ourselves in the railed field beside Sharp's, at one time.) I set Liz home. I went to bed at 7 a.m. "full weary and sore at head." The headache had been dreadful the earlier part of last night but went off somewhat later. We all enjoyed ourselves thoroughly in this outing.

*   *   *   *   *

Got up at 11 a.m. Quite well, thank you. The Dinner was a great event. Goose and plum pudding. "Very nice Mrs. Taylor; did you make <u>them</u> yourself?"

I went to see my Liz. There was nothing astir on Xmas day this year. I cuddled Liz until 10 o'clock or after and thus ended our Xmas day.

December 31st. (Mon.)

Snow! Every thing was beautifully white and "cad" as ice this morning. The day is waning. Everything is purely white & deeply blue without and roaring fires within. God Help any poor people who may have no habitation on such a cold night. There are lovely bells ringing over the water. Bob won't get down the gun till a moment before time and now 'tis 4 minutes to 12. Here comes Mrs Lizzie (Noble) Taylor. Just as the year is dying.

*   *   *   *   *

January 1st. (Tues.) 1895.

The Dinner was a success I think. Liz and I went for a walk in the afternoon. It is quite winter weather, with snow crunching beneath our feet and icy tickling sensations in the prominent parts of the face. Liz was teaching me dancing up the lane this afternoon; I think I'm awfully stupid at the art. Liz has waltzed with me before, but in a different place. Ada and her beau and I had tea together at home (much to Mrs. T. Taylor's – junior's – annoyance, as all the family were there) – whilst Edward slept. He was up soon this morning, poor soul – 11 o'clock!

The Sunday School Teacher's "At Home". I went to find Liz at 1-30, and we went to the "At Home". It was a splendid success. I almost forgot the details of the evening's enjoyment. There was dancing, of course; but the games were very good although at intervals, they flagged. Liz thought 'twas a pity everybody was looking; we could not do anything further than look at each other. Some of us, at 9 o'clock, went and brought up the piano from the Wesleyan Chapel, on a flat; and an awkward job it was. There was a singing contest between Ben Thompson and Joe Blenkinsop, which was very laughable. Ben recited a long and sickening thing too, about Rubenstein. There was some singing too. Liz and I came away with the others at 12 o'clock.

January 2nd. (Wed.) [1895]

Tussaud's Wax Work Exhibition. I didn't get up till late. I went at 11 a.m. to AH's but he couldn't come out then. He said he would go at 1-30 with me to Newcastle to The Exhibition. We arrived there with a third party and a fourth: Miss Harrison and a little boy. She went through the place with us. The figures are very good and rather lifelike as a rule, but not nearly as good as I expected to find. (I think the great fire some months ago destroyed most of the figures and these are only rushed up ones.) Most of the faces are exceptionally good: Mr and Mrs. Booth, Tennyson, the Napoleon group, Bismark, among the portraits I liked best.

The Chamber of Horrors well deserves the name. It is filled with ghastly relics of bygone barbarous ages, reeking of blood and "mare o' things baith bad and awfu' which e'en to name wad be unlafu'". Instruments of torture and modes of execution in the Middle Ages were fully carried out in reality. Blocks with victim, executioner and axe complete, scaffold, guillotines, etc. are there in all their ghastly details, figures and portraits in and on canvas of the most noted criminals are alongside of the instruments of their crimes, and engravings of a thousand different modes of torture and execution surround the rooms. Looking round these rooms and examining these different relics and portraits was fascinatingly interesting. I went to Elswick with a book but the library was closed.

Had an "at home" at No. 14.

January 3 rd (Thurs.) [1895]

Return to work much against our wills.

B. of Hope Children's evening. 'Twas something to remember. Everlasting din and yell and disorder. Some of the elder folks helped invaluably; others enjoyed themselves. After the children had passed from the well lighted and comfortable rooms into the wet slush outside, the elders enjoyed themselves, and it was very nice. Mr Walls sang, and Mr Wright, & yours truly, recited, as did Mr Jack Winship.

We dispersed at 12. I set Liz home and kissed her when I came home.

January 13th. (Sun.) [1895]

Alas! A heavy thaw set in and all day 'twas boisterously windy and raining torrents of rain.

Liz's School Exam results The Report has come and is as follows:

Infants Dept. passed "Good" (Ada);

Mixed Dept. passed "Excellent" (Mr McI.) ,

Teachers (Miss Satchwell) Excellent; Miss L. Taylor, Excellent; Miss Pugmyre, Good; Miss Buckton, Good.

Splendid, I think (in spite of the pessimists.)

January 19th. (Sat.) [1895]

Painted in the afternoon. Went to first Life class. Good model, plenty of muscle – which I like. Came back at $^1/_4$ to 8. Called at Mr Halls for a book which he had forgotten to fetch. Brought home some groceries from that mansion and got them filled up with rain of which there was abundance. Handed it in and repaired to No. 14.

Liz didn't know the meaning of the word "nude"; I referred her to the dictionary.

A man had shot himself here – and Liz's Grandmater came into the room, breathless, to tell us. I was in a fearful predicament. I was sitting on Liz's knee – so dreadful! – I got up quickly and was walking across and sitting on a chair while she was talking. I don't know what she would think! I was dubious about sitting on Liz's knee any more that night.

January 21st. (Mon.) [1895]

Bella is very unwell again, although 'tis some time since she had occasion to go to the Doctor's. Mother is all right again, but goes about too much. Went to class.

January 22nd. (Tues.) [1895]

I summed up my courage tonight and went into a hair cutting "saloon".I abhor these establishments but I must of necessity, I suppose, patronise them. Clay modelling and lecture on ornament, (Mr Pearson). Weather fine, frosty.

January 26th. (Sat.) [1895]

Went out skating and it was beautiful.

Second Life Class. Skating again until 8, when Liz and I came down. Liz got her photo taken today

January 28th. (Mon.) [1895]

Went to tea and concert tonight. Had an "at home" of an hour's duration. Snow in abundance.

<u>Fearful Row at D. E. W</u>. The Foreman Boilermaker has been found out swindling the firm, by putting in more money to a relative of his than was his due and another Blacksmith has found out and exposed the nefarious affair. The Foreman was brought up before Mr Armstrong who accused him and it was denied. However, later he has been found guilty and fined the highest penalty of the Blacksmiths Union; viz. £10. Of course, he gets his instant notice, along with others.

January 29th. (Tues.) [1895]

Row continued with alarming results and each member suffers in consequence. Mr Armstrong raging.

January 30th. (Wed.) [1895]

Mr A. in a great rage pays off the whole Boiler yard and shuts up the place, in spite of the press of work. While the Boilermen were wrangling with Mr Armstrong, Mr Archer came in, almost speechlessly drunk! After the Boilermen had left, Mr Armstrong, like a fury, turned upon him; and told him he was not in a fit condition to be in the place. Mr Archer uttered a feeble protest, and then like a vulture Mr Armstrong returned to the attack and insulted him in the most outrageous and cheerful manner; Mr Archer submitted, like a palm to the hurricane, almost without a murmur. If Mr Archer had had any pluck at all he wouldn't have entered the factory again. It looked as though he were indeed done for, but sundry persons are made to feel uncomfortably hot. Mr M. T. A. has been reduced to Foreman of Foundry and Tab shop. A new Foreman Fitter, Mr Pringle, and Mr Mc Swinburne manages boiler yards.

January 29th. (Tues.) [1895]

Liz unwell. Went to class, modelling in clay, rather interesting. Liz also has gashed her finger.

A new Foreman has commenced the Boiler yard with some of the old hands, and all is right again. Great Transformation. New arrangements, as follows:

Mr Archer, Manager of Foundry and real Store;

Mr Swinburne, Boiler Yard and Labourers;

Mr Pringle, Fitting shops. (Far too many Foremen.)

Little Albert (Bob's youngest son) in the Hospital. His right leg has never been of any use to him but they hope to get it all right there. I hope so, for he is a bright and interesting little chap; he is $1^1/_2$ years old.

January 31st. (Thurs.) [1895]

Mr Archer turns up looking somewhat the worse for wear.

February 1st. (Fri.) [1895]

Design class tonight. Came home at 9-30, or rather to see Liz. So nice, you know.

February 11th. (Mon.) [1895]

Ah! Dreadful day! Awful beyond description to that much-to-be-pitied family, Whitfield, at the high end of the village. It is a mystery why this dread calamity should have come upon this highly respected family, but we know not what a day may bring forth. May the Almighty help the bereaved one to say "Thy Will Be Done."

An explosion of the kitchen boiler, (through the fault of the pipes being frozen) occurred at 2-30 in the afternoon, in the kitchen of Mr Eli Whitfield, Whickham View, Dunston, by which his wife and daughter were killed, and two other children (one his own, the other his little sister) fearfully injured, whilst the kitchen was utterly wrecked. I saw the room a few minutes after the explosion, and I never saw such a wreck before. The Kitchen was always pretty and pleasant and happy looking; in a few moments it was transformed into a chaos of ruin. If a shell had exploded it could scarcely have done more damage. A piece of metal had got clean thro' one wall and the other walls were rent and blackened; the ceiling wrecked, the floors piled with debris, cement, pieces of metal and broken furniture, and the whole mass smoking and wet. The furniture was smashed and blackened and piled one piece upon another against the broken walls. Even the windows were shattered, and it was sad to notice the little pictures all askew and torn to pieces; all was ruin!

. few weeks later, children improving.]

115

Bessie Fox, wife of Eli Whitfield, died Feb. 11, age 29; Beatrice May, daughter of above died Feb. 11, age 18 months.

February 15th. (Fri.) [1895] Interment.

I have just seen the funeral cortege leave that house of desolation and mourning, bearing with it the soulless bodies of a mother and her child; a sad and melancholy procession with the young and the middle-aged and the old in its ranks. All alike respectful and awed as in the presence of an unknown being; all silent in the presence of death.

Her husband, supported on either side, will be now realising his loneliness as he sees the gaudy piece of earthly handiwork containing his dearest, lowered into earth and corruption, and will be only now feeling the dread agony which will make his heart desolate for so many long years to come. God comfort him! He will return with a broken heart to his wrecked home and will be tempted to rebel against the All Wise Creator – alike the destroyer of everything that is good. O, Christ, do thou prove to him a Saviour of Infinite Compassion and comfort him in this, his deep distress!

Liz & I went skating, ice in poor condition however. Liz ran away from me when we came down but I caught her before we got to No. 14. A strange thing happened after we had sat together a while. Liz seated herself on my knee and shortly after went to sleep; I wakened her but she went off a second time and slept nearly a quarter of an hour! On my knee too! Liz was quite shocked when I told her, or rather when she discovered it herself. 'Twas no use her trying to deny the awful truth or make excuses. 'Twas very nice while it lasted, but I couldn't kiss her for fear of waking her; she sat very quietly, and at 10 o'clock I awoke her with a kiss. She won't do it "no more" though, she declares.

February 18th. (Mon.) [1895]

Grand Performance of Handel's Oratorio, "Messiah".

The choir, slightly augmented, sang the choruses, and they sang them all in excellent style. Mr W. J. Plettes, Tenor, sang the solos with much feeling and his voice was very fine, (although some didn't like him.) Mr Geo Scott sang the bass solos and he appeared to be well taken with, (but I didn't like him a bit). Soulsby was asked but as he wanted a £1/1/- . (The others came for 10/6 - they didn't ask him – altho' he was miles ahead of Scott.) I believe the performance was a thorough success. Mrs. Foggin sang the contralto solos. She has a very beautiful style of singing and clear articulation, and was well received. Miss Emma Wheatley surpassed herself in her sweet thrilling notes, if not in keeping good time.

The takings amounted to over £7. Expenditure £3/10/-.   P r o f i t over £3/10

February 23rd. (Sat.) [1895]

I am an awful bad riser; nearly lost the boat, this morning. Painted a corner of our own front room this afternoon (for class). Went to Life class till 7, when I came to see Liz, as I must needs do.

February 24th. (Sun.) [1895]

Mr John Maddock suffered today from a stroke of paralysis. Very serious case.

Incident: Tim Chator and Jos Soulsby.

Tim: "Whe'as that lass Johnnie T gans with; she seems to be a very canny girl." Jos: "So so". Tim: "I divven kna what in the world she sees in him."

March 6th. (Wed.) [1895]

Weather fine, roads dirty. Davies, (D. E. Works) paid off this morning. Poor chap! He has had an awful time of it up there among those sharks and snakes, the short time he has been there. One of the quietest and most inoffensive of men who couldn't get vexed if he tried. A man who wouldn't do a dirty action but was always straightforward in his dealings. But he couldn't manage men, he was so easy going, he was no slavedriver, therefore (in their eyes) incompetent. He was fearfully forgetful and very careless; nevertheless a decent soul and they have behaved badly to him. Armstrong has been in the firm a year or two and during that time he has sent out of the place the following foremen, besides others: Wood and Percival, Watson (and all the moulders), Dagliesh and Davies!

March 9th. (Sat.) [1895]

Class Draped Figure. Came to see Liz at 8 o'clock. Little Jenny

(Miss Satchwell) there. (Tall Jenny now– she is growing – so is her hat.) Jenny very free and mischievous, but no harm in her. Liz and I had made good resolutions; I cuddled her nevertheless.

Liz's grandfather taken ill, very serious, with Bronchitis.

March 10th. (Sun.) [1895]

Doctor called.

March 12th.(Tue.) [1895]

Liz is off school, and attending to 3 invalids. Her grandfather is seriously ill and the doctor expresses fear for his recovery. His mind is wandering and he talks continually of work matters. He tries to get up and has more than once succeeded. Liz's grandfather came to the front door to speak to me about his work; he had waited at the window until I went past, and the Doctor was much concerned about it. He has got a relapse. They have to sit up with him every night, at least Liz herself has, because her Grandmother is also very ill with influenza and her Uncle Jim in bed all day. Liz is much knocked up with all this. Besides fretting after her patients, she can't get any rest and is consequently unwell. Her mother was down a bit and promises to come again.

Liz's Uncle (Great Uncle) Jim better in about a week. Grandmother about again, although not better, in about 10 days. Grandfather still ill, but not so bad.

Liz addresses her letters from Dunston Hospital!

March 11th. (Mon.) [1895] LUNAR ECLIPSE

Got up at 2 a.m. to see Lunar Eclipse but mist spoilt everything, much to Pater's chagrin. He takes a lasting interest in all connected with the heavenly bodies. In other parts of the world the shadow of the African continent could be distinctly observed in the face of the moon.

The TURBINIA. Strange looking craft on the river today. She was long and had her sheer from stem to stern the wrong way (convex). She was painted torpedo boat color and looked like one of that tribe too, and she had a huge yellow funnel with a jet of flame emerging at the top, and occasionally, a burst of smoke or soot. There was a boat on her decks, and a search light or something of the sort forward the funnel. Her cut-water was perfectly straight and she had a most curious stern something like a clipper stem a few feet behind which the yellow foam boiled in a small mountain. She ran at a very high rate of speed, causing a headsplitting sound from her furnaces and made a great swell.

I suppose she has been built from designs supplied by a Mr Parsons (formerly of Clark's.) by a Walker firm, the workmen being sworn to secrecy. The engines according to curiously exaggerated reports are working in an oil tank, and she is said to run at the enormous though impossible speed of 40 miles per hour! Should like to see her then! She is not a gun boat, but merely an experiment. As far as beauty goes, she is extremely ugly.

March 13th. (Wed.) [1895]

Liz sent a note asking if I'd go for a walk tonight, and if I would reply. I misunderstood, although it seemed plain enough <u>afterwards</u>; I went up the lane, as she asked, and did <u>not</u> send word, consequently she did not come up at 6 o'clock and I was disappointed. Liz had liberty only till 7, so I came home and gave vent to my sorrow and chagrin in a letter to her. I hoped she might come out later. Lil took the note; she had a struggle to get in at the back. Liz tells me that she locks the door after 7 and does not answer when anyone knocks. However, Lil persisted, and Liz and Jen (Miss. T. who was there for some time) gave way. They opened the door and gave Lil a specimen of Liz's handiwork in the shape of a piece of cake she had baked, in return for the doubtless–welcome letter.

March 15th. (Fri.) [1895]

I saw Liz this morning. She looks wearied and sleepy; she doesn't get proper rest just now, poor dear.

March 20th. (Wed.) [1895]

Wrote letter to Liz which A. Hopper didn't deliver; but which she got next day. I went to see Liz at No. 14. It was raining slightly, but what of that? Hadn't we been parted for three days? The gamp and my coat protected us.

We came home at the usual time.

March 21st. (Thurs.) [1895]

The weather continues fine, but boisterous at nights. I miss Liz very much. Class as usual.

March 24th. (Sun.) [1895]

I went to Liz's. Her mother came in to let me have a look at her. She appears to be a happy, goodnatured soul, stout and genial and always laughing with "sparkling" eyes, such as Liz herself possesses. She is as shy as Liz <u>used</u> to be when she saw me.

April 3rd. (Wed.) [1895]

Chapters of Accidents. During the last few weeks the following accidents have occurred at D. E. Works:- Harper Boilersmith Head split.

Coulson Hand badly crushed

Lawson Fitter Eye injured

Taylor Driller Finger taken off

And now, poor Jack Pattison who married Miss Atkinson only recently has had his Right eye so dreadfully injured that it will most likely have to be taken out. Very dull day. Intended to go to Newcastle to buy something for Liz's birthday; hadn't the slightest idea what to get though. I suddenly remembered however that all shops are closed on Wednesday afternoons, so I had to put off till Saturday. "At home" tonight.

April 4th. (Thurs.) [1895]

Liz 18 years old today. Wrote a note to her (no poetry!). I wonder if she is in any way changed; I think not. My Liz will always be the same dear, loyal, affectionate little friend to John.

The GREAT GAS SCARE. Such a Farce! I can scarcely keep from laughing as I write it! As I went to class tonight I tread, unconsciously, in some water containing some sort of tar or tank matter. Messrs. Wilkinson, Wild and Tourtel sat together in the room for Architecture, besides myself. The door and windows were closed and the gases were burning. Mr Wild began to sniff. "What a smell of gas escaping," he said, and we all agreed that the gas must be escaping somewhere for the smell was very strong. So Mr Wild got on to the desk and carefully held a lighted taper round all fittings and pipe connections, Mr Wilkinson did likewise, later on, and Mr Tourtel ditto later on again. Then we opened the door, and

Mr W. thought the smell wasn't so bad. However, the gas (where one of them thought he detected an escape!) was put out. Mr White, coming in, was struck by the strong smell of gas also. Mr White showed us through one of his notebooks and kept us in that room till 9 o'clock.

When I came into the house at night, someone, and then all, detected a strong smell of escaping gas. Then it dawned, or rather flashed upon me – it was on my boots!

April 5th. (Fri.) [1895]

I went to work in the same boots purposely, and in a very short time (after Joe & Ismay had discovered it), Mr Dobeson comes out, and, without any warning, broke out into a torrent of abuse. "Why haven't you the gas turned off – It is? Nothing of the kind. Don't tell me – Get it turned off at once !! How can it be off!!!!" (Tries himself – gas turned off already!) "Well then, it must be in the store." (Marches into the store and makes it hot for the storeman who retaliates with a vengeance, and after suffering much abuse, convinces Mr D. that the gas is really turned off. (It turned out that both were wrong!) Mr D. getting desperate now rushes back to his office and triumphantly lights his gas! Collapse of Mr Seymour – storeman for the moment. He then returns to store and finds that the fitting shop gas is still on. Mr D. pitches into him a bit more and then he (Mr D.) comes in through our office to his own, sniffing and smelling.) "Dear me! What a smell! The gas is still escaping." (Gets lighted paper, after calling us all stupid asses etc., and tries all the gas fittings.) Does not discover an outlet, but afterwards decides to send for the plumber – whom I am to bring. He twice got on to our desk with lighted paper and was each time foiled.

I had frequently to withdraw for fear of exploding with laughter! (Mr D. went to Newcastle and returned at 2-30.) Come in smelling again and remarks that the smell is "something awful." (So it was although we had the door wide open!) He had brought in Pringle and both agreed that the plumber must be sent for. I went into Watson's office to do some work and had to skip when he came in (I didn't want to go into detail with him.) – and had to go into Mr Swinburne's to finish some work. The lads didn't discover any smell, but presently when Mr T. M. A. comes in himself, sniffing as though he had a frightful cold in the head, they find out with him that the gas is escaping.

Tom Archer swore that it was escaping from the store up through between their table and the window, and as the Storeman came upstairs just then, (unluckily for him) but luckily for me. I escaped and left them arguing and jabbering with Mr S. about the evils of sitting in a gas laden room!

(I had to hold my sides with laughing so much, it was so comical.) Stanley saw me escaping and also burst out laughing and had to explain all to Watson.

The farcical comedy came to an end when I told Mr D. where I thought the smell must originate, and after he had smelt my boot (!), I felt happy for it had been a very trying task for me, to keep it in all day. Mr D. did not say much (he had said far <u>too</u> much in the morning), so he was very quiet now, merely remarking that "He was sure <u>he</u> thought it was <u>gas</u>." (!) I had to explain it all to Mr Wilde at school tonight and then there were smiles.

April 6th. (Sat.) [1895]

It was beautifully fine this morning. Very windy, but remarkably clear. You might see, except for bends in the river and bridges obscuring the sight, miles and miles of view. The quay is always a scene of busy activity and there seems to be always a vast number of vessels. Among those that ply regularly is a large iron sailing ship, which I have often noticed. Her tall and graceful spars overtop the tallest of those ships around her and her light colored sides reflect a pure white from the sun's rays. The river, rolling restlessly, a mass of feverish and slimy grey matter, is a scene of continual animation. Large vessels rend the air, and the "ear", with thunderous booms of their steam whistles and small traders shriek with earsplitting strain, and go puffing along, full of importance as the leviathans about them, which lying like huge blocks of houses topped by intricate scaffolding behind the grimy tugs, wait for the nuisance of a swing bridge (a magnificent work of art & a marvellous piece of mechanism, for all that) to toll its funeral bell, chain back its people and its policemen, and swing on its mighty axis, so as to allow them to pass on, under that towering fabric, the High Level Bridge. A perfect picture in itself and full of symmetrical grace and majestic proportion, on their way to that skeleton of woodwork, the staithes, where lie, sometimes ten at a time, and even fourteen, other ships from all parts, to take aboard their "coaly" cargo.

I went to Newcastle to school Furnishing Co's and after visiting other places, got, for my Girl's birthday, a volume of "Whittier's

poems". (Whittier is her especial favourite.)

April 7th. (Sun.) [1895] PALM SUNDAY
A pleasant Sunday afternoon. Went for a walk with Liz and then we returned to their home, where I sat on the sofa and she on my knee nearly all the night. Liz's Grandmother is poorly again.

Moon most marvellously marked. The moon shone like a silver disc, round which was a broad belt of pearly green, growing brighter and more brilliant towards the outer circle till it ended in a most remarkable russet green, almost inclined to a red; round this again was a ring of violet; a ring of yellow and then blue again, in fact it was a brilliant rainbow encircling the moon for a considerable distance all round. It was a most beautiful sight.

April 11th. (Fri.) [1895] GOOD FRIDAY

The weather looked somewhat threatening all day but no rain fell and it was never the least bit cold. All the forenoon I was busy with my dress. At 12 o'clock I went up to the school where others had been working like slaves, arranging the platforms etc. They weren't allowed to enter the schools before Friday. They had to pay 25/- (!) for the school for the single day. The little waxworks (Red Riding hood, Miss Muffett, Jack Horner, etc. etc.) had a rehearsal and then we had ours. It took me a long time to dress, but I was ready before the platform was completed. Plenty of spectators to criticise the first parts. Dinner at 2. Went to school before 3. The Darlington Sketch party opened with an entertainment of a rather comical character and then the tea was ready. I sat at our table (all tables given free) next to Liz, half in mid-air. The Darlington People had 3 performances, Felling folks two, called "Living Pictures." They were excellently arranged and well got up. The lights produced by Mr Ogden's lantern heightened the already splendid effects and made the pictures look extremely well. The Felling friends were evidently practised hands at this work. The Bigger Waxwork folks gave one performance before the Felling people, and appeared to be well taken with, and a few of ours and part of the Felling folks gave a combined entertainment to wind up with. The Characters in our set were as follows:

1 Pygmalion and Galatea W. Dixon & Liz Pugmyre
2 Hamlet & the Ghost A. S. Hopper & Jno. Taylor
3 Night Ada Taylor
4 Morning Bella Ellis
5 Queen Mary & the Executioner
      Minnie Taylor & Walter Whitfield
6 Florence Nightingale & the Wounded Soldier
      Lydia Sharpe & Dick Taylor
7 Britannia Sallie Lindsey
8 Ireland Sallie Hopper
9 Scotland Mag. Arkless
10 Portia Lily Taylor
11 Jack Crawford Alec Blenkinsop

I think that all (except perhaps the Ghost) did their parts very well indeed. "Pygmalion & Galatea" were capital, though the gentlemen made a slight mistake the second time. (Liz looked lovely, and so I have heard others say, like an angel – I am so proud of it.) "Hamlet" was first rate, "Night & Morning" well got up. Queen Mary's dress was good but the executioner rather stuffed up looking. Miss Nightingale and the soldier I did not see; from all accounts they did their parts well. The emblems of our country were particularly pleasing, and the music played suitable. "Portia " looked very nice, but Lil's voice scarcely sounded like as if it was in connection with a matter of life or death. "Jack Crawford" nailed up the Colors in fine style and was well clapped. By this single day's work with very little preparation, almost £46, clear profit has been realised. (Entertainments, £8, which is ridiculously wrong; Tea. £20; the other is made up of donations etc.)

April 16th. (Tue.) [1895]

Easter Tuesday Painted in morning. Went with Liz to Washing Well Woods again in the afternoon. We had plenty to eat and indeed, ate all the time; we climbed about too, and at last ensconced ourselves in a cleverly constructed little bower on the highest bank; in fact Liz almost lay in my arms, and while we remained here we were delightfully happy. We rambled about a good deal and did not get home till 6-30. I went across at night, and we ate nuts and sang national anthems till 9. Till 10, we embraced each other.

April 19th.(Fri.) [1895]

Sensation in our house today. An old woman who used to live in one of these streets some years ago by drink came to brought to the workhouse. She used to visit the village on her days out. Sometimes she came to our house. Old Irish Kitty came today before 11 o'clock. She seemed much exhausted. She said she had been ill with bronchitis and was not yet quite well. She had evidently been hurrying here. She asked for a drink after she had been in awhile and had spoken to a neighbour who as in with rent, and after drinking said she felt better. But she suddenly fell forward, and, striking the door with her head, slipped to the floor, where she died of heart's failure a few moments later. There were the usual crowds, later on, and policemen etc. (there was no inquest) and funeral etc. There are three people died today or yesterday and today. Oxley at Farm being the 2nd. and 3rd. a girl named Fulthorpe (Anchor Inn).

May 2nd. (Thurs.) [1895]

Did not get from work till 5. Got up to school warm and flurried at 2 to 6 and commenced

Exam for Shading from Cast (Advanced). Very difficult. Some got very little done; some were finished in the 4 hours; I only got 2/3 of mine finished. I can't hope for much; I expected to get more done. Hoping for the best

Sat 5th. May [1895]

Exam for Drawing from Life. I arrived at school in plenty of time. Model (easy attitude) (easy that is, as regards himself) posed for 4 hours – 6 till 10.

Frequent rests; which were deducted from our time. Just finished at 10 – did not get the legs "faked" much – but I think I did a good drawing – never did a better in my life, I mean in my existence (not Life drawing!) Wild thought it was Excellent. I saw Wild's and Tourtel's but none of the others to examine much. Wild did not get on so well, I thought, as last year – he did his in charcoal. Tourtel got on very well, but it scarcely looked right in every way; he does not love this kind of drawing. (I did mine in pencil – shading in fine lines and taking care to keep all the different planes plain!) There were 6 of us, in following order: Taylor, Tourtel, Sebastian Gates (the catholic priest), Nicholson, Snee and Wild. We got our positions by choosing a paper each. I was 3 rd .

Liz actually came to meet me, dear little Spartan.

May 5th. (Sun.) [1895]

CHURCH PARADE Chapel crowded.

Bandsmen played inside (sounds harsh). Ogden surpassed himself; text of his sermon "Honor all Men" and the choir sang the Hallelujah Chorus beautifully.

May 9th.(Thurs.) [1895]

Father received a present this morning in the shape of a wondrous story book from the Editor of the "Chronicle", dated "Xmas '94"!

Band of Hope Committee meeting and free tea. Helped to light fire for Boiler at 5-30. Went down at 7-30. Waited till 8-15 for Walls. Liz is a good beggar for Bethesda Chapel. Meeting till 9-30. Teacake supper till 10. Trio (AH, Liz and I) walked for lanes. Smoked. Talked of Sallie H. etc. Mr Hopper gets contract to paint Flour Mills outside and inside. Good Contract.

May 10th. (Fri.) [1895]

Managers' meeting of almost weekly occurrence. There was one tonight – Ada had recently received a letter couched in somewhat threatening terms, from the managers, who wished to remind her that the children had not to be punished other wise than with the hand (a complaint having been made by a gentleman to the effect that his child had been several times "severely flogged"). There were also other things to answer for. Ada went and demanded the reason of the letter; she did not know of any child having been "severely flogged", nor could not understand the other charges brought against her. It turned out that it had been Mr Wright who had complained of his child being punished and the other things were mainly to keep those things in her mind etc! I am glad to think that Mr Winship stuck up for Ada and he said he was glad for the way in which she stated her case and defended herself Mr Walls thought that it was quite right that teachers ought not to use any instrument of punishment to unruly children, but that they ought to be "struck" with the palm of the hand, on the palm of their hand.

May 19th. (Sun.) [1895]

Wrote a note to Liz saying I would not be at Sunday School. I could not get off going with Bob to the Hospital where little Albert is with his poor little leg which does not appear to be getting any better, although it has certainly improved since he went – 4 months ago. He has himself grown considerably and seems in excellent health and spirits – can talk and laugh and swear (in his native tongue) and is supremely happy and contented. He will not suffer anyone else but the nurses to take him out of bed and is most jealous if they handle any of the other children. He did not weep (far from it!) when we came away. It is a bright cheerful little place, is the Hospital.

May 20th. (Mon.) [1895]

Modelling Design Exam; miserable day for an exam. I got away before 3 and we commenced work at School of Art at 4 o'clock, I being a few minutes late. We had to design a piece of scroll ornament with a simple border (panel) 6" broad ? 18" long. Others did another similar thing, drop pattern. We got out at 7 until 7-30 for something to eat. After that the time flew with flying feet and 10 o'clock came all too soon. We had worked 5½ hours yet it only seemed like 2½ hours. We all got on very well in the modelling.

May 27th. (Mon.) [1895]

(Whickham Hopping.) As I soon discovered when painting in one of Hopper's fields tonight. I was wondering where all the people were going. Had many spectators and admirers. Ben Thompson and Bella promised to hurry up Liz if they saw her, but she did not arrive till nearly 9. We had a nice walk.

June 15th. (Sat.) [1895]

Painted sky in my picture this afternoon. At 8 o'clock I went and called on Liz. She followed me up. (I follow her!) We went up into the fields past Copelands. The lovely sunsets of late have stirred my soul. I am resolved to try a dab at some of them in a picture. I have thought of a cornfield for a foreground – or a harvest field in reaping time, with figures and sunset. I think I can manage. Liz and I found out a secluded little wood at the top of some field and at the bottom of another; but as we had seen some lads in the other night – or near it – we did not go in tonight, but sat on the railings. WE did not loiter in coming down as we had heard the town clock striking ten (coming down from the fields).

I forgot the fact that Bob downstairs has coughed has put me in mind. A Calamity has overtaken that gent. He always was unfortunate I think. He has three already and here's other two children for him. <u>Two</u>! I can say no more. May they both go to Heaven soon, and be put out of misery. But that's what they said about me when I was a few minutes old, a miserable looking little bit of human nature; if I had died, what a loss the world sustained would never have been known.

<u>PRESENTATION OF AN ILLUMINATED ADDRESS AND A PURSE OF GOLD TO REV. J. W. OGDEN</u>. It was certainly a splendid meeting. Notwithstanding the fewness of the people and one where enjoyment and pain were curiously commingled. Mr Anthony Hopper took the chair and Mr Whitfield was on the platform also.

Messrs Hopper, Whitfield, Thompson, Winship and Walls spoke, besides two other strangers, all testifying to the power which Mr Ogden's preaching had had upon them. Mr Hopper was, as usual most laughable, but woefully ignorant in eloquence and politeness. But he went on very well, poor man, and kept the audience in constant laughter all the time he was on. The Choir sang an Anthem and a glee. Mr Whitfield made the presentation, and Mr Ogden replied, evidently much affected, in a few words. He repeated his sincere sorrow at leaving the village and the people, and said that the Address would be the most sacred heirloom in his family, and that it would be prized by his parents. That his children would be taught to reverence as they grew up the splendid work of art which would ever be a memento of the happiest years in their father's life. As for the purse of gold the people might be assured that he would value it at 10 times its actual intrinsic value as coin of the realm. He accepted these beautiful gifts as from the hearts of the people of Dunston Church and they would ever be cherished by him in grateful remembrance. There was a good deal of hand shaking and bidding of adieux as might be expected. Mr Ogden invited Liz and I to Durham first holidays. (The value of the money from Dunston alone was £9 odd. Messrs. Geo Whitfield, Geo Noble, and Thos Taylor collectors.) Mr Ogden has been appointed to Durham. He had to go to Stafford first but got changed.

AH and I took up the Illuminated Address, by Mr J. George Hall. It is, as Mr Ogden said, a work of Art. Nice harmony of colour; every letter clearly shewn, and quite readable, framed in a brown and gold frame.

AH & I went for a walk afterwards.

Half-day holiday on Tuesday 24th June.

Liz and I took some refreshments and went into the Washing Well Woods where we – or rather I had a row with an impudent keeper, whereby I felt much humiliated, and as it is painful for me to remember it I will pass on.

It did not spoil our enjoyment however.

July 1895

Monday was hopping day; a great day – but not so great as I used to be at one time. We went for a walk – " far from the madding crowd's ignoble strife" and came down before 10. It rained heavily at intervals when we ensconced ourselves in Murphy's "roundabouts cars" till it faired. I took Liz home at 10-15 and came back myself, where, with others, I enjoyed myself with cocoa nut shorting and gallery shooting etc. and other harmless amusements. The ground was fearfully moist.

Many calamities has occurred recently. A labourer named Sloan committed suicide by hanging himself yesterday.

Two accidents at D. E. Works.

Three new nieces – two of one family: Ada & Minnie.

Bella very poorly and knocked up. Bob is growing thinner and beginning to look older. The heavy work at Derwenthaugh is too much for him. Pringle (D. E. Works) has promised him the first constant job (although he has set two other men on for a time). I hope Bob will get a better job here.

Got a canvas at Birkitts for my portrait, which I painted (5 hours) on Saturday afternoon. Walk on Sat. night.

Mon. 7th July [1895]

Liz much troubled about going away to stay for a week & being parted from me all that time.

July 14th. (Sun.) [1895]

Wrote a lengthy letter to Liz tonight, expressing my feelings toward her.

July 16th. (Tues.) [1895]

Raining in afternoon. I lived today, hoping for tomorrow, when Liz comes home.

July 17th. (Wed.) [1895]

I saw Liz on the boat at 4-30, and I longed to embrace her. Couldn't do anything at home till I got across at 7-30 to see her. Strangers have no business to hear or see what we said or did on that happy night. I was in the zenith of my delight. It seemed as though a month had elapsed since I clasped her neck and felt her cheek against mine. We were rather late in separating.

July 18th. (Thurs.) [1895]

I took the portraits across for Liz to look at, AH would not stay or go for a walk so Liz & I stayed together.

July 20th (Sat) [1895]

Soliloquies by J. T.

I think I must be far too ambitious. At present I am weaving ambitious schemes in my brain; I have not time for anything, only an hour or two a day; I am getting far too old (am nearly 20!) and want everything done at once. I want orders for portraits; I have done my own and have nearly finished AH's. I think Mr H. wants me to paint Sallie's! I believe the Foreman boilermaker at D. E. W. also wants his likeness painted, I wonder how much they think I ought to charge? That is most important. An artist's price for his work seems high but he must have payment for his art education and for all he has expended in colours & brushes & canvases beforehand; "there's the rub." I want a landscape painted and the Summer's nearly gone and we are not having very good weather; I want to paint Minnie's portrait and I want to paint Liz's portrait. In other branches I want to get some black and white sketches done to send to papers. So as to "get on" as I hope to sooner or later. Also, in an entirely different art I want to write and illustrate some stories for submitting to different editors, and the best of it is – I fancy myself quite able to do it all! Poor ambitious self! And yet I will try to do it all. I hope although I have only got a second for "Life".

Well, and so it is Sunday August 4/95. & I am still wondering what has occurred last week worthy of note. Will Maddock has gone from our Chapel to Gateshead (whatever will Ada do, poor girl). The schools had about 5 weeks holiday, but got started last Tuesday. Liz is really thinking seriously about putting her hair up off her shoulders!

Notes for week ending Sat. Aug 10/95. Wet first part of week, but beautifully fine after Wednesday – rather cold at nights. Went for walks or across the road every night during the week. On

Thursday night we sat on the cut stump of a great tree in the "Forest" and whispered.

Wages now £4-15-0 per <u>month or £1-2-0 per week.</u>

THE DIARY
Volume 4 - Sept 1895 - 1900

It is now September, 1895 AD. The weather, on this particular Sunday is delightfully fine – "but watery looking," according to the Prophets. I hope not. We have had far too much wet recently. It was very fine last Sunday for the M. N. C. Sunday School Anniversary. Today is the second day for its Celebration. It was quite nice last Sunday, (although Dunn did not turn up.) (How those bells of St. Stephen's chime! It reminds me of Sunday mornings long ago (I am not an old person) when I used to be taken by my mother to "Old Thompson's" before going to Chapel. He died some years ago now, poor man of a broken heart through being removed from his old cottage. I used to stand on the Quay (Dunston) and think St. Thomas's tower with its four spires was a huge stool standing with its legs in the air!)

Last night (Sun. 11) [1895] I set Liz up home (G'head.) She goes to Scarborough on Monday.

Exam results – Liz gets a 2nd. at last for Freehand.

Exam results – Yours truly – I scarcely dare say it. I have made an awful muddle of it all. Two failures, two Seconds, one First!

How shall I escape? And outline drawing not accepted. What a take down. And yet I can explain it all. Anatomy – I had only a week's notice and did not expect a First – thought I might have got a Second. Of the lot who did Modelling design on those two fateful days. Only two got Seconds, I not among them. In Elementary Water Color Design three of us got Seconds, the rest failed. I, drawing from Life, I can say no more than that I was astounded and mortified at only getting a Second.

On Tues. 20th. Aug. [1895]

The watchman got a weeks notice, for doing nothing wrong. Of course it is the rule up at D. E. Works now when they rid of a man to send him off without excuse. Geo Gladson is an old man; he has been sent out of the place to go for all they care, to beggary or want; they do not know his circumstances, nor do they care. The Foreman

Boilersmith had missed something from the yard belonging to the Hydraulic Rivetter, and said it had been stolen. Mr Swinburne, full of business, of course blamed the watchman for not attending to his duty in watching the place. Next day, after they had given him a week's notice, the cap was found where some of the fools had left it or dropped it. One would then naturally have thought that Swinburne would have apologised or at least cancelled the Watchman's notice; nothing of the kind. Geo had also asked for an advance a week before, so this became Swinburne's excuse for getting rid of him. Another man had sometime ago been appointed for his place so the thing was all cut and dried. Old Johnson, the new man, used to stop Mr S. and tell him tales (to which Mr S. like a gentleman, listened!) about the Watchman. So they worked the thing so cleverly with their lies; (Johnson's son-in-law, Tom Swaddle is a labourer at the Works and the two of them seem to have concocted the vile plan between them.) With the result that Gladson has been put out and this other old rogue put in his place. I wonder Swinburne did not burn to the bone for so unmanly a trick to be guilty of. Of course it is only one more dirty trick to the credit of that already thrice mean firm. What did they do to these foremen who have gone before, to Jim Wake & Davies, Foremen over Fitting shops; to Dagliesh, Foreman Pattern M.; to Watson & Gray foremen Moulders, to Harry Wood and to Tom Smart Foremen Boilermakers (of course Percival F'men B'maker deserved his notice) and what have they done to Simpson whom they appointed at a certain wage and have now reduced? Oh! I am sick of at this infamy and treachery, and now Pringle, the only man among them all is leaving, for a better place; perhaps he is sick of them all. He gave Bob (brother) a job at last. I trust he will stay there. (Only Pringle made a mistake in not giving him the highest rate, which I hope will soon be remedied).

Poor Brother Bob. On Fri. 23rd. one of his twin babies died, and within the week the other had been buried. He has certainly suffered, poor fellow, and has been most unfortunate.

October 6th. (Sun.) [1895]

The Big Fire at the Mansion House. By which Henzell's Oil stored in the old Newcastle close Mansion House was destroyed, besides a great quantity of timber owned by J. Herring & Co., and other damage to various property. We all went along to see the flare up. Every possible point of vantage was lined and crowded with thousands of spectators whose faces were lit up by the fiery glow of the flames. The sight of the fire was terribly grand. The lurid flames rose high into the black night, towering over the high roof of the old Mansion House and enveloping it in wings of fire. Only two thirds of the back ruined wall is left of the Mansion House now, and the scene presented is one of complete devastation. The timber was a roaring mass from Davisons Flour Mill on one side to the Oil works on the other side. The firemen were on all sides, and worked with great zeal and perseverance – of course it was of no use pouring water on the flaming oil, but in keeping the flames from spreading to the oil works on the left side, nearest the High level bridge. For hours the flames burnt fiercely with unabated fury. On Monday night when I went to class there were still plenty of spectators to see the flame and smoke which still made a comparatively good fire!

Biggest fire since 1854 Hallgate Explosion.

October 20th. (Sun.) [1895]

Brother Bob gets on badly with Shaw (manager) who is as useless a man as could be found. He expects to be paid off next week when the ship "Chipchase") is finished. He has been living in hopes for 2 days on chances of getting the appointment at the flour Mills but alas! – to say the truth – he is fated to disappointments; he has been born under an unlucky star. Of course he has much to be thankful for, health and strength etc. etc., but all the same poor soul! He has suffered much since he was married.

October 18th. (Fri.) [1895]

Hamlet (Mr and Mrs. Burbohm Tree)

I went to see Hamlet. (Lasted over 3 hours.) I do not profess to be a critic or a judge of these matters, but I really think that the company could not have been excelled, for the excellent manner in which they carried out the piece. Hamlet was a fair Hamlet; he had a peculiar voice, but very powerful and thrilling; his acting was simply perfection; it seems he has quite an original manner of treating the piece; he treats some parts almost lightly. I fancy the way in which

Tree tree- ted this part, the words themselves in the part of Hamlet's pretended madness are light and frivolous; and a lunatic is not always sad – oftener delighted. In the "Play" scene whilst, Hamlet watches from the opposite side of the room, on the floor, the faces of the guilt-stricken King and Queen he crept the full length of the stage until he was underneath their eyes, and the expression on his face was one of such realistic triumph that one involuntarily put down the glasses amazed. At all times the expressions on Hamlet's face were terribly real.

Ophelia was splendid, more especially in the part where she is roughly treated by the would be mad Hamlet and also when acting the part of the demented Ophelia; the piece where she brings in the flowers being most touching and deeply pathetic. The King and Queen were capital actors. Horatio good, but scarcely so well up as Laertes, (Ophelia's brother) who went about his part as though it were a stern reality. Polonius, there never was a better, a real old man, an old man's actual style of talking, of walking, and of bothering people! But who can forget these grave diggers – clowns as Shakespeare calls them; they were clowns indeed! The rest of the characters with the exception of the play King and Queen and the ghost, were somewhat amateurish, that is compared with the exceptional brilliancy of the greater stars.

Lily was celebrating her 17th. birthday tonight after the fashion of young ladies by bringing lots of folks to tea and supper.

December 24 1895

On Xmas Eve Ada and Minnie and I had a rare old meander; the rain and wind swished like a pelting hurricane loaded with shotcorns, and underneath feet, all was delightfully soft and quite bottomless. Nevertheless, braving the storm of blustering wind (the sleet <u>did</u> cease, somewhat!) we faced its wrath. I bought some things for other folks whose friendship I could not exist without, It is so pleasing to reward others; you feel that at least it in some measure atones for your unknown other hypocritical actions; most of us, however, are far too closefisted, alas. I <u>did</u> see Liz too, tonight. Pater likes "General Gordon" which I managed to get for him, well. Bought a <u>bag</u>, at the suggestion and choice of Ada, for Liz, with which she is <u>delighted</u>.

December 25th. (Wed.) Christmas day [1895]

(10/- from Mr D.). Got up at – ahem! – 1! Dinner at 1-30. (Nothing stirring today.) Was over road good part of day, also seeing AH, who had several friends seeing him. I took across a canvas and sketched in a portrait of Miss. P. in charcoal. I needn't prophecy; by the time I am writing this from my notes, I have almost finished a good likeness (so she herself says) – only it is somewhat solemn and sedate, for my vivacious little friend.) Liz is delighted with the "thing " I bought for her.

December 26th. (Thurs.) [1895]

At work this morning. Holiday afternoon. Painting Liz's portrait.

Liz cannot sit at her Exam for the Scholarship, through some mistake; she is bound to be in agony, poor dear, but she does not show any thing. There is nothing so courageous as a suppression of feeling, especially in a woman. She is a heroine in a small way, is my dear Liz.

(Later: They have managed; Liz is to sit.)

(Later again Liz sat – a hard Exam, but hopeful.)

<u>Lil</u> has not done so well as the others at the Exam, and is comfortless – just now.

* * *

January 17th. (Fri.) [1896]

At Mr Youngers nearly all night – gossiping. <u>Liz jealous.</u> I am busy painting my lady's portrait, which I can candidly say is by this time (end of Jan) a fair good likeness. Liz is very much pleased with it. She is teaching me to dance now. I am afraid I make a very elephantine show. Last night, for instance, I came from class; nearly 9 o'clock it was before I got down, and as I had travelled through roads such as (Hercules's) waggoner would have died on the spot had he beheld, my feet were not exactly in a <u>presentable</u> condition, much less for dancing. So after our preliminaries (I am not going to state in black and white exactly, what <u>they are</u>!), I took off my boots and I fancy Liz in a state of utter exhaustion after she had hauled me about for 5

minutes. I feel like a bear on a tightrope. She fancies now that I can –
I dare not say it. Perhaps I will get better.

Yesterday Brother Robert was paid off – for a time I suppose.

January 28th. (Tue.) [1896]

My darling Liz, the Good Samaritan.

What a pleasure – what an honor – to be acquainted with one, no
matter how humble, who is always ready and willing to help a fellow
creature in distress. Without any one else but recipient knowing of
the good action, a man or a woman who does another a kindness, to
his own or to her own inconvenience – is the noblest of creatures.
How few of us do such an action; we are all for self and let everybody
else look after himself – even the helpless. Most of us are too much
filled with self esteem and greediness for ourselves to mind our
suffering brother.

January 29th. (Wed.) [1896]

Sk. Club meeting at "Pavillion Café". I took Liz's portrait. It was
well received. Mr W. praised it very highly and said it was a decided
improvement on AH's. Mr P. thought the colouring was excellent. In
fact I was quite astonished at the general good opinion of it

February 5th. (Wed.) [1896]

Enjoyable evening. Dancing with Liz. (<u>Good</u> dancer now!) Bought
Liz gloves, for the Teachers Social (Ball, I ought to call it).

February 17th. (Mon.) [1896]

Explosion at Whickham Colliery; 2 men killed, 2 men injured. Poor
Liz ill several days with toothache and sleeplessness. Lovely weather.

March 20th. (Fri.) [1896]

Choir Social – or rather dance. It was all dancing nearly; as I
enjoyed myself immensely. Of course Liz was there, and Jenny
Satchwell.

March 23rd. (Mon.) [1896]

Lovely weather, almost warm. I see Liz every night and every
night I fall in love again; she is a most loveable creature; so happy, so
good and so pure and high minded, and of a most forgiving nature,
she forgives me much too. But she has suffered a good deal recently;
she is waiting of the result of her Scholarship Exam. I expect she will
get a first; she and others, a second. Of course I can't comprehend the

difficulty of the thing. I only have faith in her powers.

March 27th. (Fri.) [1896] Liz has got a First Class Pass!

She came across to our house this morning and asked for me; her face was beaming and she handed me the big envelope, but I knew it was all right. I could have cried with delight. The dear girl has won her honors; she has expected less, waited patiently and borne the suspense bravely. Everybody who hears of it is highly satisfied.

May 10th. (Sun.) [1896]

I am glad and relieved beyond belief. The worst Exams; viz. P. of Ornament and Architecture are over; Friday & Saturday last saw them carried off. I may get seconds! For the Life and Figure Design Exams last Saturday and Monday I won't be surprised if I get firsts. I was particularly happy while doing these. I have the Modelling (Muddling) Exam the week after next; it is a long, but an interesting, one. In the honors stage, I and Mr Wild selected the following: "A male slave, front view & side view, supporting Ionic Architecture". Mr Pearson did "Man struggling with death (skeleton) with decorated border". (The other I would have done but forgot the meaning of the word "Mural". It was to be a design in a triangle, representing St, Martin (Roman soldier on horseback) dividing his cloak with the naked beggar.)

Sunday. I got the Life Exam over last night (Sat. May 2. [1896]) in (to my mind), a most satisfactory manner; it was a very correct drawing and boldly executed, so far as I am able to do, it is the best I have ever done. On Monday first I have my Honors (Design Exam) to look forward to.

June 23rd. (Wed.) [1896]

Ada and Maddock and Liz and I go to

Tynemouth. Rained until we got there, and then it was fairly fine until we came away. We were at Whitley, most enjoyable.

June 24th. (Thu.) [1896]

Liz and I at Elswick Park, seeing the statues etc. Splitting headache. (Little Cissie very cross today, poor dear, alas for what happened.)

June 18th. <u>Hilda Mary Hall, 4$^1/_2$ years old died June 18th. 1896 at</u> 9 o'clock in the evening. The sunshine and the blue sky are glorious without; but within, all is blackness and woe. There is a sound of lamentation, as of Rachel weeping for her children which are not. How shall we face this awful reality? Hilda dead! A chill shoots through the frame at the very thought. Poor Little Hilda! The sun shines and the landscape is smiling with beauty, but the little one is gone from us. So vivacious, so bright, so full of life but yesterday; and now–

O!– God the merciful, God the compassionate! Send comfort to those whose affliction is as wormwood. Heal with balm those wounded hearts, for Christ's sake!

She was a strange little girl, much too wise for her age; unlike other children she was not always childish; she seemed to have the mind and thoughts of a grown person. At times she was so serious as to frighten those who saw the little face rigid and thoughtful, with her great blue eyes full of tears, as though she saw things not of this world. And so, in the midst of life – like a tiny flower which has shed abroad its fragrant odour and given life and sunshine to those about, and which is now to be gathered in as to great a prize for the good Gleaner to lose – she has been taken from us, and those with whom she came in contact are sorrowing and sad in the bitterness of their bereavement. The good Lord has taken her to be forever with him and we shall see her hereafter; she is not dead, but gone before.

As I long as I live I shall never forget the agony of the bairn's poor broken hearted mother; it was a sight to soften hearts of ice. Everybody in the room where the coffin lay, was weeping; all except Kate herself. She seemed unable to comprehend what was happening and sat gazing into vacancy until they were screwing in the screws and then – God Help her – I think she went mad for a time. But now the wounds are healing; God grant it may be so. The memory of that sad Sunday with its bright sun and glorious landscape will always haunt me, and the sound of the Sunday School scholars singing "Glory,

Glory, Glory!" Nothing ever sounded so sweet or so sad, or so terrible. Hilda is now at rest and her childish grievances and little cares are banished from her. There is something beautifully childlike in her last few words – "I'm going to thleep, Ma – Giv's a tiss. Good night Ma!"

Alas! This is not the worst. God have mercy upon us!

On July 2. [1896] Thursday morning at 1 o'clock, poor Hilda's little baby sister, died of the same fell disease, exactly a fortnight after, and now the only comfort poor Kate and George possessed is also taken away. Cissie (Isabella), age one year and one week, was buried last Sunday (July 5 th) in Hilda's grave. O! how terribly cruel! What does it mean? O Christ thou Comforter, who sorrowest with thy people and who rejoiceth when they are glad, have compassion upon us and give us consolation in our bereavement!

Kate & Geo are staying through the day at our house for a few weeks.

July 6th. (Mon.) [1896]

Sent story to W. Chronicle for competition. Title given "Cruel as the Grave". 1500 words.(hon'ble mention July 18/96.)

July 9th. (Thu.) [1896]

Liz went to Cullercoats (55 Eleanor St.) to stay with Satchwells for a week or so. Sorry that it rained, especially at night. I mean this in both ways; I was especially sorry that it rained at night because I couldn't stay out for a walk by myself and had to come in soon like a wandering sheep.

July 11th. [1896] (Sat.)

Ah! How I waited and longed for this day. I went by train to Cullercoats. Liz, alone, was waiting for me. I could have smothered her then and there with kisses, but of course, there were other people. She looks better for her stay I think, though she says I made her want to come back to Dunston. We wandered all over the place, the three of us: Jennie and Liz and I. What a little tease and a pest Jennie is. She is always shy or modest, an expert climber of rocks, sharp with her little feet, sharp with her tongue and quick to perceive. She is a most lively companion, especially when she sits on top of one, and is particularly endearing when she rams corn stalks into your mouth and ears, whilst raining blows on your shins with your own stick. There was some damage done to dresses, for which, of course I will have to take the blame. I was very sorry to come away; those who know me will believe this if they believe nothing else. We trio sat upon a porters bogie and Jennie would push us all over the platform on it, and at last ended by putting her feet up on the same level as she was sitting herself, sitting thus until train time. I got a good seat and Liz bid me goodbye again, her eyes very bright.

July 12th. (Sun.) [1896]

Liz away. Very lonely tonight. Wrote a letter to Liz in the "Wonderful Forest".

July 13th. (Mon.) [1896]

I asked for an advance last month and, as the year was up, have got 4/15/- per month just now, or 22/- per week. Hope to get 25/-. Did not mention what I wished for. Alas for hopes of successes!

Results of Exams as follows, (so far):

Life Drawing: Wild, Taylor : second class; Nicholson: fail.

This is two seconds I have got; Mr Wild has 4 or 5! Nicholson passed 2nd. last year and failed this year!

Modelling & casting Heads: Wild: first (Hear Hear!); Pearson: second; Taylor Fail (hear hear!!) This speaks more eloquently then comment. I have all my pride knocked out by this time. I feel floored. Whatever will the results of my other three be? I wonder if the missing off of the plaque (to which the head was fixed) could have anything to do with the fail?

Five-Day Trip to London. We left Central Station at Midnight

August 2nd. (Sun.) [1896]

Slept a little. Train ran pretty fast. Stopped some time at Grantham. I believe it was at Doncaster early in the morning where we saw a curious effect. The whole countryside – green fields and trees – was bathed, several feet deep, in pure white mist which gave the effect of a hurricane snow storm in summertime. We arrived at King's Cross Station at 8; and at our lodgings (not without considerable trouble) at 9 or 10. We arrived at the Royal Academy at 11, where we stayed till 5 (this was the last day of the Exhibition).

Writing now, over a week after, I seem in such a whirl with having seen so many thousands of pictures and works of art; I seem unable to remember distinctly what I looked at in particular places. The Academy pictures, which I saw for the first time, appeared to me to be up to perfection. I never dreamed of anything like it. I may be pardoned for mentioning a few which I remember. Lord Leighton's was much admired – unfinished – and so was poor Sir John Ev. Millais's (died a day or two ago) . A man called Godward took my fancy for beautiful women – nude and draped. They were exquisite.

We next had a look in the National Gallery, and in the National Portrait Gallery but did not see much of them. The National Portrait Gallery, we saw most of the Old Masters. What curious ideas these old people had – and what fine and vivid imaginations. The drapery was nearly all beautifully painted and much of the flesh painting was marvellously beautiful. I think modern painters have beaten the old masters, from whom they learned the art; but the old masters will live when modern men are forgotten in oblivion. "The Old Masters" work was original; they invented the art and had only nature to study from. Walked from here to the Horse guards, Westminster Abbey, Houses of Parliament, down Thames Embankment, passed Cleopatra's needle, and St. Paul's Cathedral in the gloom; returned by Fleet St, Strand and Piccadilly. Arrived at lodgings 10-30.

After letters were written, bed at 12-30.

August 4th. (Tue.) [1896]

Took underground train to Blackfriars Bridge for St. Paul's Cathedral, arriving 10-30 am. We looked through the aisles and nave. The dome is beautifully painted with 8 paintings by Sir Jas. Thornhill, all of St. Paul's acts. The monuments to heroes which took our fancy were those of Wellington, Nelson, Gordon; the latter a beautiful black marble tomb with an effigy of the "Bayard of the 19th. Century" on top in sleeping position. We did not see the Painter's Corner where Landseer, Turner, Reynolds, West, Opie, Leighton etc. are buried. Collingwood, Picton, Napier. We went into the Whispering Gallery. The paintings by Thornhill are not about much; appear very rude. Left the Fire Monument, from which we obtained a fine view at 1 o'clock. Magnificent view of London from here. Miles upon miles of houses! Went to the Tower where we stayed till 4-30. We were much interested here, looking through the grim relics of former grandeur, and gazing upon the names of princes of goodness and martyrs to faith engraved upon the timeworn walls. It makes me shudder to look into some of the dismal places, dark and dank, but what would they be like in the days of Bloody Mary and cruel 8th. Henry? Within the walls White tower, some of the blackest deeds in English history were committed. Here within these terrible walls have been incarcerated defiant Elizabeth (as a Princess) by her cruel relative Mary, and poor little Lady Jane Grey by the same unnatural woman; the one to return to might and glorious deceit and power, the most unfortunate one to the block.

Here gallant old Sir Walter Raleigh was imprisoned; here the courageous son and knavish father – the Dudleys – were confined, and all at length suffered the terrible penalty of their genius or unfortunateness on the scaffold. In the Wakefield Tower they keep the Regalia in a strong iron cage.

In the upper rooms of the White Tower is the block and axe which executed Essex – the Elizabethan favourite – and Lord Lovat, the last victim in 1759. There are piles of torture instruments, suits of ancient and modern armour, old guns, muskets, pikes, swords, arbesques, rifles, bayonets. I think the hundreds and thousands of arms and parts of rifles, swords etc. which decorate the walls and ceilings of many apartments are given by the Government when obsolete. The Tower is also quite a museum of foreign arms and weapons, especially from India and China.

We came back by London Bridge where we saw more then one of the proverbial black and white horses. At 5-30 we took underground train at Mansion House for Earls Court Exhibition, arriving at 7-30. Stayed till 11-30. The place at night presented the appearance of an Arabian nights Palace, with millions of bright white lights. The exhibition which we went through was A1. They had an enormous quantity of paintings and sketches in watercolor by Carpenter, they were exquisite; and magnificently done. There were also very large paintings of Hindu subjects; and grand paintings they were, quite equal to the best Academy work.

India Exhibition.
This was certainly the most delightful thing I ever saw, with regard to entertainment's there were <u>hundreds</u> of performers on the stage at once. The play was made up from Indian History from the time of the Maharatta time up till the crowning of Queen Victoria, Empress of India. The building was very spacious, the seats systematically arranged; the lighting excellent and the acting, which mostly included dancing (there was no speaking, except singing of chants etc.) was up to perfection. The scenes of the girls dancing by the riverside (a lake under the stage, which was composed of sliding boards;) the lovely scene in sunset light and moonrise light, the brilliant colours; the sweet cadence of songs, weird & wild & melancholy, was at once enthralling and startling in its splendour. It reminded me very forcibly of the description in the story of "Aladdin & the Wonderful lamp". A most marvellous and wonderful entertainment (by Kerfaldy).

Brought some presents at Earl's Court(pipe, brooches, purses etc.). Stayed until 11-30. Got underground train back to Victoria Station. Arrived lodgings 1-15 a.m. Wednesday morning.

August 5th. (Wed.) [1896]

Started out ¹/₄ to 9. Went through Hyde Park, Rotten Row, and admired Albert Memorial, the most splendid monument in London – perhaps in the world – built by public subscription. The mosaic work is like a series of paintings; and the sculptured work, both in bas relief and otherwise, is magnificent. I have got some photos of the groups. (Tom and Ed missed a great treat by not seeing this monument.) Went past Albert Hall, Museum etc. and entered South Kensington Museum, first looking through the <u>Exhibition of students' works</u>. There were some beautiful works of art in all its numerous branches (water, oil, crayon, pencil, black and white – design, figure, flowers, birds, animals – sculpture and bas relieves etc. etc., most of it up to a high standard of excellence). Saw some of the antique head's (Voltaire's) which I did not get through in. I could have sworn one of them was mine; only mine had no plaque behind. (I wonder if that had anything to do with my failure? This fault just struck me there. I thought my work very good – as I generally do, of course – that's my misfortune!)

But here another and more forcible surprise awaited me. In entering one of the little partitions on the walls of which the works are hung, I suddenly saw a most familiar piece of my own artistic labour. I had been anxiously awaiting the result of the Design (Honors) Exam and had not the remotest idea of how I had got on. (If I ever thought of passing the idea of the fail for the antique head floored my happy wishes for success.) There then was my work marked Class 1 st . I took it as quite natural, for fear Geo might think I was excited;  but I could not restrain a little exclamation, impressive of delight. There were three subjects: A -Soldier & beggar; B - Skeleton and man struggling; C - Slave and entableture. The exhibits were as follows: three of A; two of B; (one or two) and one of C, which was my own.

I felt very proud. I feel delighted even now, for I have had confirmation that the drawing was really mine, and that I had actually got a first. (You think I might have been mistaken because no names were shewn? Not I. I knew my work the instant I saw it.) I am sorry to say that both Messrs. Pearson and Wild did not get through in this. Anyway, it is quits for the Antique Head work. Have got a second for Architecture; Nicholson, regret to say, failure. He has come on desperately bad this time. We are both looking forward to the Bewick Club. I will not say anything more about my pleasant discovery at Kensington, but that it was a most happy one for my trip to London. Looked through the other things in Kensington and left at 4-30. Geo has a note about the Chicken Rissoles we had for tea. I don't like to think of them again! We passed Olympia, and took tram to Crystal Palace. Arrived too late to see much. 8-30 and stayed till 10-30. The Palace looked somewhat melancholy from the outside, but there was a little life inside. Bought some things inside.(Band played a bit outside and it was well lighted.)

Some trouble with Railway trains coming back. Got back at 11 p.m. Took "bass" at Hyde Park Corner. Walk down Piccadilly, Strand, Fleet St, had supper and returned by bus to Sloan St. Got to lodgings after the usual trouble (finding the right place – in fact Thursday night and Friday morning were the only times we went straight to them) at 1.15 a.m.

August 6th.. (Thurs.) [1896]

Bus at 9-30 to Burlington House, Piccadilly and looked through Diploma and Gibson Picture Galleries. Here was a most magnificent collection of the work submitted by the painters to gain the R. A. since the commencement of the Academy. 11- 12-15. Walked through and bought some things in Burlington Arcade. Walked down Regent St., passed Duke of York's Column (a standing disgrace to the nation, and to a wicked and useless man), Horse Guards etc., and went into Westminster Abbey, mainly to look over and find the burial places and memorials erected to the honor of "The Illustrious Dead". In this great, solemn temple of God, with its towering columns and overhanging roof of beautiful workmanship, with the soft lights of every hue filtering through the stained windows – standing as one does, over the ashes of heroes and saints. Looking around to find the effigies and tombs and memorials to a hundred giants in the Arts and the Sciences; in the Arts of Peace and War, one feels a thrill of awe and an overpowering inclination to do homage to the mighty dead. To William Shakespeare, to John Milton, the prince of poets of his day; to Rare Ben Jonson, to poor Gay, to the inspired author of the "Elegy", to that unfortunate mixture of wickedness, genius, and genuineness, poor Rabby, and to scores of others equally worthy of being remembered by the nation of which they were so proud.

There is a bronze bust to the "Bayard of the Nineteenth Century" – Chas. Geo. Gordon, somewhat unimposing; but nevertheless, a reminder of the most forcible kind of the Noblest Christian of his day; who lived a saint and died a hero. If the brotherhood of American and Englishmen needed any further demonstration, it is to be found in Westminster Abbey in the busts to two of the finest men of this Century - Longfellow & Lowell.

(12 till 1-30.) Left Westminster Boatlanding for Greenwich Hospital at 2 o'clock. An hour later got to landing. We met two Dunston men here, or at least one Dunston man and a Blaydon man. We went with Arthur Blenkley and his friend (both still speaking

broadest Tyneside) through the room where The Nelson relics are kept. Here we saw the frock coat that the great little man wore and the short uniform coat that he wore when shot at Trafalgar. The coat does not look particularly old even now – 91 years after, though of course the stars and decorative orders are faded and tarnished; yet the cloth looks good (policeman blue). There are numerous swords and medals and guns that he received from various persons, and letters etc., also a lock of his hair and pigtail tied with a bow of black ribbon – the hair which is of a very light golden grey, is as fine as silk and more like a woman's than a man's.

The great room in which these and other things are shown is hung with hundreds of portraits (and a valuable art collection it is) of Captains and admirals from Blake and Hawke, and Sir Cloudsley Shovel to Collingwood, Howe, Nelson, etc. and up to the days of the Crimean War. There are portraits of Captain Cook and a picture of his murder. Some of the greatest of the naval fights with the French are depicted by apt hands and one feels, as in the solemnness of Westminster Abbey of the Dead, a reverence unknown in other Galleries, a deep feeling of thankfulness to these great Britons of other days, some of whom in their day were the despised of those whom they defended, and some of whom were lauded to the skies, but all of whom did glorious worth against our hordes of enemies to uphold the honor and the courage of their native land. Honour to the brave! The ceiling is decorated and painted in a most splendid and gorgeous manner by Sir Jas. Thornhill, which must have taken several years to accomplish. The room is called the "Painted" hall, and it is well worthy of the title. It is an Art Gallery as well as a place of interest. Came away before 5. Got back after refreshment at 7-30. Went to Houses of Parliament at 8, with tickets procured by myself from Sir Jas. Joicey (made mine out to Mr Sayer). Stayed till $^1/_4$ to 12. Saw several big guns. Saw Salisbury in going in – Chamberlain, Balfour, Goshen and others of note. The business was uninteresting, but there was a good deal of disturbance and Dr. Tanner (for calling "Hear Hear", after called by the Speaker) was severely talked to, but shortly after left the House. Walk through Strand, Fleet St, then by Pall Mall, St. James' Palace, Piccadilly and Hyde Park Corner, arriving home

1-30 Friday morning.

August 7th. (Fri.) [1896]

Lodgings at 9-30. Bus to Tottenham Court Road, changed for Regents Park, and & after much bother arrived at 11-30 at Zoological Gardens. Got sketch of lion. Most interesting sight to see the animals and birds (and parrots and monkeys). Left 3 o'clock. Bus to St. Martins lane, by Long Acre to Trafalgar Square, arriving at 5 o'clock. I stayed here intending to have another look around the National Gallery before leaving London – a look until 7, while Geo left and went over London Bridge way with the intention of buying some photo he had before seen. Judge my keen and bitter disappointment when I found the place marked (Close on Friday 5 o'clock!). I had either to hang about for 2 hours or go after Geo. I followed the latter course but did not fall in with him. I was back before 7 and he came a little later. We got bus to Hyde Park Corner, and arrived at Lodgings at $^1/_4$ to 8.

We got something to eat, settled our bills, had a bit chat etc. and left at $^1/_4$ to 9. Got bus at Sloan St. for Kings Cross Station (passed Marble Arch on way). We fell in with our friends who accompanied us to London. They were very jovial. We all got into the same compartment again and they had a rare old time of it coming back. The journey home seemed shorter, though it took exactly the same time as going. I got some sleep.

We were dreadfully funny on getting out at Newcastle Central. Eyes sandy; morning air cold; generally queer etc. Got home after a struggle, I was thoroughly awakened when I got home on

<u>Saturday morning 7 o'clock</u> – 30. Talked and had breakfast, showed what we had brought etc. and after that I went over to see Liz (took her Handglass) about 11 o'clock. Sleepy over there. Smoked. Asleep at night, much to the amusement of Miss Liz. Was very submissive.

August 29th. (Sat.) [1896]

(Holiday from work for men's trip.)

Went with AH and saw Caton Woodville's Splendid picture: "Battle of Doornkop – and Dr. Jameson." New hat.

A young girl called Maggie Lawson died recently after a painful illness; well known in the village; there was a very large funeral on the Sunday.

October 19th. (Mon.) [1896]

Bewick Club. On Monday night (having got official word from the Secretary in the morning) I went by the 6-30 boat to Newcastle – I met Nicholson at the Bewick Club entrance. We went in together. They would hardly allow us to go up into the Life room, and remained dubious until we saw Mr. Ralph Hedley, who appears to be a particularly nice and kind individual; he squared matters and we went in. The nude female Model was posed. She is very beautiful, like a picture almost; and has a splendid head and handsome face. I got on very well. There were only 8 of us present. Irving (Chronicle Artist) and the two Wilds were there. Saw Liz at night.

October 22nd. (Thu.) [1896]

Bewick Club. Male nude – same model as School of Art (Weatherslone – Cavalryman), who is a capital figure. Worked hard. Still somewhat strange of course. Good job Wild and Nicholson are there. Poor attendance at nude classes evidently.

October 23rd. (Fri.) [1896]

Bewick Club. Old man – fine, military looking – with flowing white beard, in mendicant attitude. Ralph Hedley's "Veteran".

November 1896.

This will be a famous month ever to be remembered in history. Before it has been completed I shall have reached the crisis of my memorable history. I shall be a man.

November 10th. (Tues.)[1896]

Bewick Club tonight. Old man. Mr R. Hedley said my work was very good. Showed me something tonight. Offered to lend me the coat (his) which the old man has been wearing to finish from.

November 27th. (Fri.) [1896]

This day has at last arrived and is now on the wane. I do not feel any older; but at the same time the terrible fact is a fact– I am arrived at maturity. It is a sore point with me so I will not discuss it.

Presents: (!) Liz: pocket case made of leather – beautiful;
Ada: yellow kid gloves;   Bella : Silk Tie;
Maggie: pocket book;   Stanley Silver links.

AH (dear old boy): a 22′ Palette of Spanish Mahogany.

Little party to tea on Sunday following. First time Liz has had tea in our house, I think, at least with me.

December 11th. (Fri.) [1896]

Lovely Dance (most beautiful.)

New (about 6″ high.)

Xmas and New Year.

The holidays were very quiet. Photographing and eating Xmas puddings and sweets and geese, sending cards, opening letters etc. etc. Thus the day was spent. Painted part of day.

January 16th. 1897 (Sat.)

Painting at new picture –"Interior"– all the afternoon. Lost my stud at night and Mrs. Hopper found it. Liz is in love with my new photo.

January 28th. (Thu.)

Liz wept a little tonight, I forget what for. She has got some extra <u>grant</u> today and is excessively happy. I think that must be the reason. I had no class tonight. She had misunderstood Ada's intentions in giving her an extra amount of grant. She has bought a great many presents.

January 30th. (Sat.) [1897]

Was going to do some <u>skating</u> today there had been skating all the week – but a fresh set in and did for me. The Bewick Club is at its wits end. Another large deficit this year. I am getting on exceedingly well at the Bewick. They are somewhat stiff; I must pick up what I can.

R. Hedley is very kind.

February 6th. (Sat.)

Black and White sketch of Cromwell's time.

February 26th. (Fri.).[1897]

At St. John's Dance in Newcastle. Schoolteachers and Maddock and I were there, being invited. It was a superb time - the recollection of the beautiful floor is like a dream. Everybody was happy.

July 26th. (Mon.) [1897]

Sent following pictures to Lamesly Exhibition. "Judas", "Traitor" (Black and White), "A little Alien", "Landscape", "Portrait of Artist".

July 29th. (Thu.) [1897]
At exhibition, AH and Liz etc. there also. Was disgusted with the way they hung my pictures. Impossible to see them. They were flat against a partition dividing a narrow way where two streams of people were passing and repassing. AH brought them back a day or two later.
(Salary 5-5-0 to 5-15-0 month, 1-4-3 to 1-6-4 week, 69-0-0 year.)
July 31st. (Sat.) [1897]
Seeing Lund's picture of Elswick. It is a very fine work, exaggerated and made <u>into</u> a picture but clever, though not a remarkable work.
August 21st. (Sat.) [1897]
Choir Trip to Stocksfield. Fine weather. Enjoyable trip. A few good painting subjects. Saw through the gardens etc. and old Castle. Photographed complete. Got back late.
September 9th. (Thurs.)
Liz and I and Geo H. and Kit went to see "Midsummer Night's Dream," and surely, in the history of the stage, nothing was more magnificent then the scenery and the dresses of the actors. Everybody was delighted.
September 28th. (Tues.), 29th. (Wed) [1897]
Lettered Boiler; Hall Brothers. Another "nowt job."
November 7th. (Sun.)
My poor dear friend Andrew Hopper taken seriously ill with Typhoid Fever. I was to see him tonight. He is fairly better, but has suffered much and appears very weak.
November 11th. (Thu.)
Was off work today. Bro. Edward married to Harriet Grey (Ettie) of Gateshead this morning at 10-30, at St. Paul's Church, Gateshead. Yours truly was best man. It was a very pretty ceremony; but withall a shabby finish. We do not know much about Ettie. She is somewhat distant and uppish. She is pretty though, and nice enough when talking to one. I hope they will live happily. They are gone to Edinburgh on their "honeymoon"(whatever that may be) for a week.
November 27th. (Sat.) [1897]
I am 22 today. Reflection on a growing evil is to sad a

contemplation for me. I have got a tie, a handkerchief, from Mag and Ada, a volume of selected poems from George, and, last but no by no means least, a "Byron" from Liz.

December 24th. (Fri.) [1897]

At Newcastle buying presents for Liz, Mater, Pater, and Minnie.

December 25th. (Sat.) [1897]

Xmas day, I believe. Quiet. Up at 12-30.

December 28th. (Tues.) [1897]

Tom's Social (towards New School) made about £8. At Tea somebody threw a biscuit and struck Liz on the face. I thought it was A. Brunswick and asked him to apologise. He was very impudent and unmannerly. I was boiling with rage & stormed and threatened. Then one of Dotchin's (who had done it) came and apologised. That was all right I told him, but I couldn't get over Brunswick's boorishness.

December 31st. (Fri.) [1897]

Firing guns etc.

The usual annual merry party. Jack Noble etc. Tom's first foot.

January 1898

The D. E. Works Company, always the same, still behaves shabbily to its clerks.

January 28th. (Fri.) [1898]

Ada's operetta with Children in Board School. Took £11, expenses £2.

January 26 th (Sat.) [1898]

Laying Foundation Stones of M.N.C. Lecture Hall and Sunday School. The day at first fine then windy, at Stone laying a deluge of rain. Stones realised £190-10; tea 7-18-1; Ceremony collection 5-4-4$^{1}/_{2}$; Concert Collection 5-7-10$^{1}/_{2}$. Concert on good scale at night. Speakers: Rev. Allwork from Whickham, Enoch Hall, Jobling, Ogden, etc.

March 4th. (Fri.) [1898]

Bewick Exhibition of Members works very good. My portrait is hung. Mentioned in W. Chronicle. At B. C. Conversazione after Collage.

March 13th. (Sun.) [1898]

Up seeing Edward, with Liz. I often wonder if Ed and Ettie agree well. She seems very nice, but she doesn't appear to me to be cut out for any man's wife.

March 28th. (Mon.) [1898]

Liz has her room to her self now. Her Grandmother's brother has left the house, and not before time. He was an able-bodied man and never worked. Let him work now, instead of living on the earnings of a young girl.

March 29th. (Thurs.) [1898]

Liz is afraid to go to bed. She is lonely.

April 4th.(Tue.) [1898]

Liz is 21 today. Got many presents. Is much older and more womanly.

April 10th. (Mon.) [1898]

Dance. (Ambulance Association.) It was very nice. Liz enjoyed it very much, so did I.

April 11th. (Tues.) [1898]

Poor Andrew! How can words express my unutterable sorrow to think that my poor dear friend, the friend of my former years with all his great weaknesses and all his great goodnesses – is dying. Going forever from the earth. I cannot realize anything so awful. It is beyond comprehension. It must be impossible! He was up at the Bazaar for a few minutes. How pure and deathlike he appeared.

April 24th. (Sun)[1898]

Tom was up seeing AH yesterday and he is much the same, a little better then he was through the week. He has a nasty cough which, though not frequent, is very painful when it commences. He was quite cheerful and happy and spoke of coming back home next week. Poor dear lad!

April 29th. (Fri.) [1898]

Andrew came back from Gillsland today. He is looking remarkably well just now (end of May), a month later, and is a cheerful as he could possibly be, in the best of health. O how glad I am. To think that my old friend may yet deceive the doctors.

June 12th. 1898

LIZ! O my love! How sweet she is; how blessed it is to be beside her. We are always together every night but we still long for the time

when we shall be together for better for worse!
She is going away for a whole fortnight I'm
sure I don't know what I shall do all that
time. I cannot bear to think of it. I hope she
won't be miserable or I shall be so too. I
hope she will be happy and enjoy herself.
God Protect her and Bless her. Make me
more worthy of her; make me good enough
for her and we shall be forever happy!

June 15th.(Wed.) [1898]
Man committed suicide on the
railway at Dunston.

June 20th.(Mon.) [1898]
Launch of HM Battleship Albion
on the Med. Fearful loss of life. 34
bodies recovered, caused by the wave of
water, sweeping away the staging.

June 27th. (Mon.) [1898]
Liz goes to Newbiggin for fortnight.

July 2nd. (Sat.) [1898]
Went to see Liz. O the rapture of that blessed day. To see my love
again!

July 3rd. (Sun.) [1898]
I don't know how I spent it or how the time has passed. But here
is Sunday again (10) and I was seeing the dear child again yesterday.
Like a fool I got out at Newsham instead of Bedlington and got to
Blyth, from which I walked by the seaside most of the way to
Newbiggin where I found my sweetheart. O how these two weeks
have dragged on. How lonely I have been! What would it have been
like had it been 2 years or even 2 months! I think I should never have
been resigned. We have been very fortunate, Liz and I; I hope we shall
continue to be so. I have written letters and kissed her photo until it
is spoilt with the moisture, but O for the <u>reality</u>. Newbiggin is a
delightful little place, with sweet salt sea breezes and strong fresh
gales which send your blood tingling. They have a lovely landscape
and seascape down there; and Liz says the sunsets beat anything she

has ever seen. She will be home tomorrow night (July 11), and then I shall make up for lost time!

Liz looks very pink and has immensely enjoyed her stay; in fact says she would like to stay another week! Ah me! And I? Whither shall I go? Mrs. Kent and the children has evidently benefited by the holiday too.

Andrew is very ill again poor old chap; at frightens one to see him so pallid and racked with a hacking cough. O God! Be good to him, be good to a good soul!

June 30th. – July 5th. [1898]

Maggie, Ada, Lil and Min Hunter at Valances, Edinburgh. Liz and I went to meet them coming home, and we all saw Sarah Bernhardt arrive at the Central Station.

July 27th. (Wed.) [1898]

Minnie and Lil went to tell Ed; and his wife (our dear sister! Save the mark!) of the glad tidings of great joy (the latest arrival – Rena Margaret Hall, age 0), but as Ed was out, <u>Ettie could not under any circumstance allow them to enter, so they had to came away again</u>!!

<u>LONDON August 1898</u>

August 1st. (Mon.)

Academy 11-30 a.m.-4 p.m. Lodgings – Tea – Band on Embankment 6-7.30, Empire Theatre at 9.

August 2nd. (Tues.)

Whitehall – St. James Palace. National Gallery 12-2.30. Boat to Chelsea – Carlyle's house – and Dante Rosetti's house. To Earl's Court, the 2 Toms came to meet us here at 9.

August 3 rd (Wed.)

Went to Thrush St. to see Isabella. We all bussed to London Bridge and went to St. Paul's Cathedral 11-12. British Museum 1.30 – 5. Stayed till 11 at Thrush St.

August 4th. (Thu.)

So. Kensington Museum & Natural History Museum 9.30-4. Albert memorial etc. Geo left us. We went and sat in Hyde Park and then to Thrush St. till late.

August 5th. (Fri.)

Strand, Westminster Abbey, Trafalgar Sq., Went onto St Martins le

Grand Church. Spent afternoon in Oxford St. Strand and lodgings.

We had splendid weather; but for my part, I did not see so much as last journey, mainly I think of account of the unwieldiness of a party of four (George, Tom, Tom Junior and I), all of different inclinations. Young Tom soon tired, although he seemed to enjoy everything. The charges were fairly reasonable at the "A Home from Home"; but I'd rather have been at the old place in Chelsea. O <u>how</u> I enjoyed the Academy and the National Gallery with incalculable wealth of works of Art. Those pictures of Turner are fascinating, such divine coloring and realism as I could find in nobody else's works.

Isabella – poor dear soul – has come back very ill indeed, and is in bed for four weeks, improving very slowly. Dr. Dougall is attending her. The journey must have knocked her up so she did not enjoy herself much.

August 19th. (Fri.) [1898]

Weekly Chronicle Competition for Illustration of Local Anecdote. I got 2nd. Prize 10/-.

August 20th. (Sat.) [1898]

Passed 1st. for Life.

A Great Idea. The new lecture has a great white expansive wall at the W. end; and I have got myself possessed of the notion that I can improve it with a large religious cartoon. As it is the Sunday School, what more suitable subject than "Suffer little Children".

August 18th. (Thu.) [1898]

I was hearing General Booth, speaking at Gateshead, High West St. Chapel. He is really and truly, a grand old man; he looked splendid in his dark blue uniform and red jersey; with his grand characteristic face and long silver hair and he spoke very well. He preached a wonderful sermon from Revelations, when he depicted the last judgement and the destruction of the world. He is not eloquent, though he is a unique speaker with a certain fascination of his own and would attract attention in any place and at any time. He is certainly worth listening to – a truly wonderful man and one of the greatest of the century.

March 1899

"His life was gentle; and the elements so mixed in him, that Nature might stand up to all the world and say – this was a Man!" Julius Caesar.

It was a long – weary – a heavy time for poor Andrew Swaddle Hopper, so long as his illness lasted – about 18 months. But he held out wonderfully; towards the last his fight with the Grim Messenger were terrible – pitiful! To watch his wasted form sitting day after day, week after week – month after month, wrapped in the great warm dressing gown, his face white and cream, his great beautiful eyes, black and burning, and sunken under his heavy white brows, his pale marble brow on which was, of yore, never a line of care and still through it all never a wrinkle, his hair long and lank and dark against the whiteness of his skin; his long pale colourless fingers clasped in his lap, O to see him it was pitiful, it was pathetic too when he talked, for his words were the words of one only ill for a time; his hopefulness was wonderful. Poor, dear, much-loved; much-loving Andrew. The love between him and his friend was wonderful – passing the love of woman. It is a long long time since I first knew Andrew when he was very small and I also was very small – but I am glad to think that the earliest recollection I have was of defending him against bigger boys who were pulling his hair. But the story is too long: I know it – in fact, it is traceable through these writings. We both of us had – have – many friends yet each of us had one friend. I thank God from my heart that ever I knew Andrew Hopper.

1899 Andrew died February 3rd. Friday morning at half past 3, after suffering dreadfully for some days. His end was peaceful and happy; the afternoon previous was glorious and sunny; the beams from the orb of day illumined the room and the bed and the pillows and his wan face; the blue shadows across the counterpane and the white pillows. The flitting of birds twittering and winging their happy flight across the sunlit window cast momentary shadows; he wished to be raised to gaze upon the glorious scene; his father lifted him and he looked eagerly and exclaimed time after time "O isn't that grand! Isn't that grand!"

God accept him! Christ receive him!

Andrew & William Brown, William Dixon and myself carried the great oak and brass coffin containing his remains. He was buried at

Whickham. When all the ceremony was done, I waited to read the inscriptions on the tokens that had been sent – wreaths and flowers; it was bitterly cold – all the vast crown melted away, and when I looked up I found myself alone – alone with my friend.

How strange and weird and cold his face was like unto wax for whiteness, and cold as marble as I kissed his brow for the last time. Good Bye, dear old man – but not forever!

New Picture in Lecture Hall.

Made sketches and commenced to paint October 1898. Completed picture December 24th. 1898, three months. (Sunday School anniversary on Sunday December 25th. and Sunday January 1st. 1899.) Picture open to admittance on Monday 26th. December. Raised nearly £2 towards cost of frame for canvas. Sunday School voted £2 odd making £4 towards total of about £5 or £6. Frame not really finished till October 1900. The picture subject is "Christ blessing little Children", the most suitable subject (to my mind) for a Sunday School. I have painted at it since first it was hung up and am now (1900 October) trying to simplify it somewhat. All are highly pleased with the painting. I regard it as a means of showing my gratitude to God and to the dear Sunday School.

Newbiggin by the Sea. 1899

I was staying here for my holiday this year. O the unutterable bliss of that golden time for Liz was there too. There are some events in a man's life that are so sacred and so divine that he had best not commit it to paper. Those days of sunshine on the moor and the moonlight nights on the sand! They will live with me for ever.

September 1899

Did some cartoons for Weekly Chronicle at 7/6 each – a very modest sum – but to much for them to pay. Dissolved with them Oct. 99. Xmas 1899 Did a cartoon £1/5/- for "Northern Gossip".

December 31st. 1899!

It is nearly a year ago, yet I still marvel at the revelation that I learned that night. O how can I speak of it. The love of my innocent Liz has been so pure and untainted that in these days (when very children eat of the tree of the knowledge of good and evil) it passeth the wit of man to conceive! That wonderful, that marvellous, that passionate, that divine love which my sweetheart bears me is a miracle notwithstanding her utter lack of knowledge of man and woman. And now, ah! Now she is a dear little woman whom I shall shortly (in a year or two) call "Wife".

God bless her and protect her dear life!

London: August Mon 1st. to Fri. 5th. 1900

On holiday. Tom and his wife, Ada and Alfie were with us and Liz was there! How sweet and delightful even to think that dear Liz has seen the great sights.

"Judy"

On August 5th. (Fri.) 1900 I took some sketches to let the Editor of "Judy" the London Serio Comic Journal, see them. Ed, De Marney is a very young man, and proprietor and Editor; He received me very kindly and liked my work very much; so much so that he told me to send up what I did. I sent my first cartoon, on my return, entitled "An Awkward Team" (having reference to the Powers action in China). He published it in Aug 29th. Issue, and since then I have had one published every week – once two in a week. The average rate is 15/-; I have succeeded in pleasing him and next year 1901 I will do one every week. It is a good beginning and I consider myself very

fortunate. It is just what I love. With Tenniel's glorious drawings in my eye I can manage very well, I believe. The Art Editor is somewhat officious, but scarcely an artist.

1903. October.

Isabella Mary, beloved sister, passed from pain to endless tranquillity in God.

[The remainder of the diary consists of accounts and family deaths etc.]

Postscript

John had over forty cartoons published in "Judy" magazine and was invited to go down to London and join the permanent staff, but the family were against it, and there was Liz who was Headmistress of the Board School in Swalwell from 1900 until she was married. John and Lizzie were married in December 1903 and at first lived in a flat in Ravensworth Road, Dunston. Here their first child Ted was born and their daughter Marian was also born there in 1908. By the time the third child Hugh arrived in 1912 they were living at 26 Johnson Street, Dunston.

John Taylor continued with his work as a clerk, he was the last employee kept on by the Bailiffs to pay the bills when the Dunston Engine works went bankrupt in 1923. Then he was out of work along with many others. He had continued to paint and exhibited frequently at the Laing Art Gallery in Newcastle and elsewhere. Lizzie organised an exhibition in 1926/7 and several of his pictures were sold but money was very tight. The Taylor sisters visited frequently and usually left a bag of food behind a chair, although nothing was ever said about it.

In the early years of the century John had been asked to tutor a young boy called Wheeler Dryden. Wheeler's father Leo Dryden was a Music Hall Singer and had lodged to boy in Dunston while he was on tour. On his return, he found that Wheeler was talking the broad vernacular, so he asked around for someone to tutor the boy's speech. John Taylor was recommended, and he worked on Wheeler's speech for some time. When Wheeler left Dunston and went away with his father on tour he kept in touch with the Taylor's. In due course Wheeler became independent and toured India and South Africa acting and singing. In the year that Wheeler was 21, he recieved a letter from his father, informing him that his Mother whom he had never known was Hannah Chaplin, and that he was half-brother to

Sydney and Charlie Chaplin!

By this time they were all in the film business in America so Wheeler went there too. At first Charlie was reluctant to acknowledge Wheeler, but later he invited him into the family and into the film world. In 1927 Wheeler had returned to England and was making films at Elstree Studios. He wrote up to John Taylor, knowing that John had no job, and invited him to come down to London and be his secretary. So the family did come down to London.

Ted worked for the racing driver Parry-Thomas; Marian went into service and eventually spent several happy years as Nursery maid and later Parlour maid for a family called Hill-Smith, at Abbotsbury near Elstree. John lived in digs at first, while Lizzie packed up all their stuff and left many pictures etc. with different relations. Then she came down to join John. Last of all came Hugh, aged 15, who had been staying with his aunts.

So all the family were in London and they settled at St. Donat's Rd, New Cross. John continued to paint lots of pictures both of scenes in London, and more "fantasy" type pictures, such as pirate ships, illustrations for books, and Christmas and Birthday cards.

On one occasion he went to apply for an artist's job, the man asked what he could paint. "I am an artist," said John. "What do you want me to draw?" "Can you draw a giraffe?" "Of course," said John. The man disappeared so John set to and drew Giraffe's large and small, single and in groups, standing tall and stooping down. After a while the man came back and said "I cannot find a picture-" and stopped amazed. He had been looking for a picture for John to copy! He took John on so that he would be able to draw the things that no-one else could!

They lived happily in London, until 1938. Ted had married by then and moved up to Luton in Bedfordshire, to work at Vauxhalls. John and Lizzie decided to move there too. They rented a house at 105 Cutenhoe Road, half way up a long steep hill on the south side of Luton.

Marian was home with them by now, but Hugh was also recently married and living in Honor Oak, South London. Their first grandchild, Hugh's daughter Anne, arrived in October 1939 and John

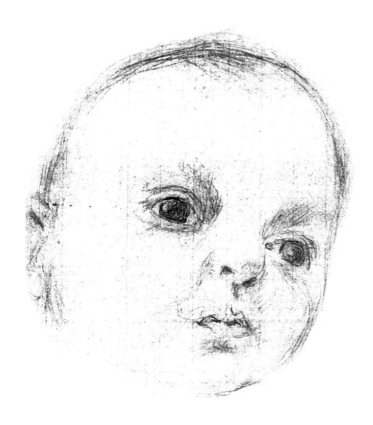

did this little sketch of her that Christmas.

In February 1940 John died in the Luton and Dunstable Hospital at the early age of 64. Lizzie and Marian ran a boarding house all through the second world war. Lizzie died finally aged 95 years still at home with Marian in Luton. John and Lizzie are both buried in the Crawley Green Road cemetery at the top of the hill in Luton, with a view over towards Cutenhoe Road where they had lived.

Anne T. Taylor.